In Wisdom's Light

A Message of Peace for All People

Volume I

Emi Miller

Cover and book design:
CreateSpace

Portions of *In Wisdom's Light* previously published on the author's private listserves.

ISBN: 0692127100
ISBN 13: 978-0692127100

Library of Congress Control Number: 2017902642
OliveTree Press, Charlotte, NC

Quotations, photography, and poems used with permission:

The Way of Life According to Lao Tzu, Witter Bynner, Copyright © 1944 by Witter Bynner, Copyright © renewed by Dorothy Chauvenet and Paul Horgan. Used by permission of The Witter Bynner Foundation for Poetry

Kabir, Love Poems from God, Twelve Sacred Voices From the East and West, Daniel Ladinsky. Copyright © 1999 by Daniel Ladinsky. Reprinted by permission of the author.

Awake Awhile, We Should Talk About This Problem, A Divine Invitation, and Would You Think It Odd, from I Heard God Laughing: Renderings of Hafiz, by Daniel Ladinsky, Copyright © 1996 by Daniel Ladinsky. Reprinted by permission of the author.

No Mud, No Lotus, The Art of Transforming Suffering, Thich Nhat Hanh, Parallax Press, 2014; Under the Apple Tree, by Thich Nhat Hanh, Philippe Ames, p. 6, 2002, Parallax Press, Ca., the publishing arm of, United Buddhist Church, Ca; Understanding Our Mind: 50 Verses on Buddhist Psychology, Thich Nhat Hanh, Parallax Press, February 9, 2002, 2006; Being Peace, by Thich Nhat Hanh, Parallax Press, 1987. All quotes used by permission Parallax Press.

Quotes of Paramahansa Yogananda, sources listed on pages, used by permission, Self Realization Fellowship, Permissions Office, 3880 San Rafael Ave., Los Angeles, Ca. 90065.

"All this world…" quote is from "Meher Baba's Universal Message; "Shun those Masters…" is from a message Baba gave in February 1966; "The Avatar is always…" quote is from Baba's "Highest of the High" message; Being Good, and Law is Good, quote is from Life Eternal, Book II. Permissions for all from AMBPPCT.

Photos: Nature's Beauty Lake and Going Up, photos by Emi Miller, permission to publish, Meher Spiritual Center, Inc

Photo: Tibetan Woman Elder, image copyright James Wheeler, 2013. Used under license permission from SouvenirPixels.com

Photo: Birnbeck pier at Weston-super-Mare, Somerset, and Quantocks, image copyright, Nick Whetsone, used by permission of the artist

For Eva Rose,
who reflects the beauty of this world

Acknowledgments

With Gratitude

I am deeply grateful to all of the Divine Masters, Prophets and Saints, followers of truth through the ages, in whose steps I respectfully attempt to tread. And for my Teachers, those who still walk this Earth, and those who have passed, I am very grateful to have received from the vast storehouse some of the Wisdom you were entrusted to carry. Many thanks to those who have let me use their photos, including James Wheeler, for allowing me to use his beautiful photo, *Old Tibetan Woman*. I am especially thankful to my daughter, Eva Rose Edleson, whose eye for beauty and whose tender heart can be enjoyed in her lovely photos that grace this book. Much gratitude and thanks to Daniel Ladinsky, for the many gifts and inspirations his poetry reveals. To Witter Bynner, and his foundation for poetry, thanks for your amazing dedication to gathering and keeping Lao Tzu's essential verses with humanity, through such a clear and profound translation. Heart-full gratitude to Paramahansa Yogananda and Sri Yukteswar, you are Divine gifts of Love to this world; and to Thich Nhat Hanh, Wallace Black Elk and Mother Teresa, who continue to help many find a rock to stand upon in our unsettled world. A big thanks to Rabbi Morton Kaplan, for his thoughtful review and praise of the '*New Yet Old Translation of the Shema.*' Thanks also to the many readers, who over 18 years have thoughtfully sent messages letting me know the daily posts have added peace and benefit to their lives. And to Eunice Paul and Evelyn Hannaman, thank you for your kind help in reviewing this manuscript. I am also very thankful to Abbey at Create Space, for her amazing patience and immense help in the designing and editing of the book. Finally, abundant gratitude to the Avatar Meher Baba. Though I became acquainted with his teachings only recently, his illumined guidance has supplied the necessary push, to bring to life the volumes of In Wisdom's Light.

Table of Contents

Introduction

The Living Transmission of Wisdom

And while I stood there
I saw more than I can tell,
and I understood more than I saw;
for I was seeing in a Sacred manner
the shapes of things in the Spirit,
and the shape of all shapes
as they must live together,
like one Being.

— Grandfather Black Elk

This first volume of *In Wisdom's Light, A Message of Peace for All People* has had a long and amazing path to reach your hands and hearts. If I were to attempt to share the whole journey that has brought this work to you, it would take an entire book, and I believe many of you would find it to be at least somewhat unbelievable, or even downright imaginative. Yet I can assure you that many blessings and divine gifts have been given to this dedicated seeker of truth, and if you choose to come along and share these poems and prose with an open heart, you will enjoy a taste of the sweet fragrances that have been captured here.

My youth was spent dealing with much illness, and so I chose to pursue and practice a path of healing. This path of dedication and seeking, studying, digesting, and finally practicing and teaching, has spanned many decades and includes both traditional and modern forms of healing. Yet side by side with this work, I was also deeply engaged in an inward journey: Seeking the roots of the world's ancient and modern religions. I was sincerely and whole-heartedly trying to find one path that would unite all people and all ways, underneath One Divine Creator. I felt that recognizing that there was only One Creator guiding all of humanity, all spiritual paths, would not only be the truth, but would certainly help to bring peace to our world.

This Inner seeking-journey began at the early age of six, like Grandfather Black Elk above, I experienced "seeing in a Sacred manner". The Earth was shown to me to have gone through many cycles of growth, over-development, destruction and rebirth. The vision was as vivid as my everyday reality, and occurred early one morning while I was sitting up, awake in my bed. I was shown that the Earth was in process of yet another of these times of renewal. Why did this occur to me? At the time, I was so young that I did not even think to question this or to speak of it to my parents. Yet, this Gift, and the knowl-edge that was given, has stayed with me since then, and has in fact guided my steps and my journey. After speaking with people over these years I have found that many others have also stories to tell about Sacred occurrences in their lives, yet like myself, they do not often share them. And so, much deliberation has gone into the sharing of this portion of my journey with you. It is a risk. And yet it may also open the way for others to come forth: ordinary people, not mys-tics, not 'seers' but people just like you. For though we may tend to believe that the ancient Prophets and Saints, and even more recent people like Grandfather Black Elk could have had inspirations and been able to see in a Sacred manner, we tend to isolate into the realm of unbelievable, those in our midst who would brave dissent and share their own Sacred experiences. My question, "Why me?" was answered only as my journey unfolded.

When I was in my late teens, I actively began an in-depth study of the world's religions, Throughout the many years of seeking unity in diversity, I found myself sitting at the feet of Great Masters and Saints from the world's religious and spiritual traditions. Then I found that many cultures held a similar view of the Earth that I had been shown in my early youth: that the Earth has been through several cycles of growth and destruction, over eons of time, and that we were now approaching another time of destruction and rebirth. Only this year have I read a report that scientists are aware that the Earth is experiencing its sixth period of extinction and annihilation. I was somewhat surprised by this announcement, yet it confirmed what I have been aware of since my youth.

In 1990, one morning, while in a deep meditation, I experienced another Sacred seeing. I call it Sacred seeing as it was so very clear, and I was actually inside, watching and learning, even though I was in quiet meditation, still sitting on my mat. In this Sacred seeing I was shown each religion having its own Ray of Light, emanating from a huge, radiant sun. Each Ray had people walking, in single file, upon it. And at a certain moment they began to move themselves, in order to form the different letters of one religious path: people walking on each Golden Ray were followers of that path.

Actually the sun was so large that I was only able to see one portion of its Rays, and after the letters were complete they spelled the names of various religions: Judaism, Zoroaster, Hinduism, Christianity, Buddhism, Taoism, Native American, Islam, and others, each on its own Ray.

Slowly, the people began to move out of the letters they had formed, and lined up in a single file again, along each Ray. As they did so, I realized that each Ray of Light was not only important for the ongoing existence of those Souls traveling upon it, but also was important for the creation and maintenance of our Earth Family, the manifested universe, and the Divine Realms. Further, as Grandfather Black Elk said, I "understood more than I can tell". And yet I can say that each Soul, along each Ray, was a living part of the Whole Being, and to deny the importance of any one of the Sacred Paths, established by the Most High, could only occur through our complete lack of understanding. And further, that war and other forms of intellectual exclusion, actually harms the integrity of all.

This was a profound experience for me. Then, all at once I saw: All of the Souls, traveling on their own Rays of Light, had their backs toward the sun— the One Creator of All. They were all walking away from the sun. Thus no one was able to see that all Souls originated from the same Source. Realizing this in a Flash of Inspiration I thought, "Oh! Everyone just needs to turn around and See! There is Only One Creator Creating All!" As this realization, occurred I suddenly began to laugh out loud! It all seemed so simple! At that moment my laugh was unlike any laugh I have had before or since. My long journey to find the One Source of All Ways had brought me to this wonderful Gift of realization. Of course my laughter instantly brought me straightaway back to present time, sitting on my mat.

One morning, many years later, while immersed in my daily meditation and prayers, I received another Sacred seeing. All at once my room became filled with light, and a portion of Wisdom was clearly brought to mind from one of the paths I had walked upon. The same thing occurred the next day and the next. Each day's awareness arrived with great clarity, and along with this clarity, I was filled with immense love. Slowly the great Beauty would retreat, and I immediately went to my computer to write what I had received. Each day my eyes would fill with tears of gratitude, for the many Masters and Saints I had been blessed with in my life and the incredible Wisdom, that had been left within each of the Sacred paths I was honored to be following.

This period of intensive work lasted about one and a half years. The poems and writing in all of the volumes of *In Wisdom's Light* contain whispers of the great Love and Blessings of that time. I have continued to write each day, and I still feel a connection to that time of wonder and Grace. My journey has led me to a wonderful realization: not only is there only One Source that has established each and every holy path, but there also has been only One Divine Message given to all people. And this one Message strongly pulses with-in the Living Heart of the followers of each and every honor-bound Way.

While most of the writings speak of love and harmony with the All-in-All, and amongst people and the natural world, some also speak of warnings for those who are in positions of power over others—in families, governments and businesses, and in particular for those religious leaders and editors of sacred texts who deliberately alter the truth, or harm the followers of their path, for their own egotistical purposes. Leaders are held to stricter standards than others.

Since 2002, one of the writings has been daily sent to several invitation only websites that I host. People join us from many Sacred traditions and beliefs, and from countries around the world. It is the desire and purpose that the poetry and prose in the volumes of *In Wisdom's Light,* will help to bring peace between the peoples and faiths of the world. As noted above, I know that many artists and others have similar stories to tell, and perhaps some will gather courage to share their journeys by reading mine. And so, for those who believe this blessing of Wisdom could have occurred to anyone in our day and age...and for those who have some doubts, but are willing to push their hold button...and for those who are unable to believe that this could be anything other than some kind of delusion...the volumes of *In Wisdom's Light* are being offered to all, with deep gratitude, for their amazing birth and blessings.

You may be wondering about the One Divine Message I found that each path carries at its heart. I will share that realization with you here. Perhaps you already have this same understanding. If not, at the end of your reading of these volumes, see if it rings true for you:

Underneath and above and throughout
the variety of different paths
and ancient texts

there is but One Source,
One Divine Song

Given to and sung by all hearts
throughout all seasons and climbs,
all cultures and epochs.

It is a song of Peace, of
Harmony and Love;

Spoken by all lips,
it Lives with-in all who have
ever drawn breath—

Love one another.
Do unto others as you would have
Others do unto you.

Do Justice.
Respect and care for the Earth.
And daily give thanks, to the Creator of All.

May all beings join hands and hearts together, so that the words of the Prophets will soon be fulfilled: "On that day, the Most High will be known as the Creator of All, and peace will reign on Earth."

—Emi Miller, 2018

Daily Meditation for World Peace

Perhaps you have a daily meditation or prayer time dedicated to peace and harmony on Earth. If not, or if you would like to have another, I offer this for your consideration:

For a few minutes each day, in mediation and prayer, open your heart and offer your thoughts for a world filled with harmony and peace. During this quiet time, try to sense the presence of millions of people who are likewise engaged from all paths. If you are so inclined, you may envision and join the Masters, Saints, and Prophets from all Sacred Ways who encircle this world with prayers for peace, both from this side and the Inner Realms. Together with their followers twenty-four hours a day, in harmony, and yet each in their own unique way, they are focusing their loving prayers and meditations to bring peace to our world.

I wrote this prayer for the Boise Peace Circle I created and led for 12 years, after the vision shared above. It is still my daily prayer. If it resonates with you, please feel invited to use it:

A Prayer for All

May all who are hungry find food.

All who are without shelter find shelter.

All who are suffering find solace.

All who are without Love, Be Loved.

Amen and Amen.

Three Faiths Declaring the One Creator

Judaism

The Shema*

Hear! Understand!
Guard these words and act upon them.
Struggle to Remember
The Divine Presence of the Universe.
Our Oneness is bound together throughout eternity.
O, remember, Divine Being,
The One Breath of the Universe. *

Christianity

There are different kinds of gifts, but the same spirit distributes them.
There are different kinds of service, but the same Creator.
There are different kinds of working,
but in all of them and in everyone,
it is the same Creator at work.**

Islam

He is the One Creator; there is no other creator beside Him.
The Most High, the Most Sacred, the Peace,
the Most Faithful, the Supreme, the Almighty,
the Most Powerful, the Most Dignified.***

---

* Translation of the Shema by Emi Miller, See explanation in appendix.
** 1 Corinthians 12:4-6
*** Qur'an 59:23

Given to All Paths All Ways

Throughout all epochs all spheres,
looking with the eyes of now
at the ending of our current era

those who can See and Hear,
and understand,

will not fail to bow down
to the Creator of All

as we peer into the Mirror
of the Ages,

and grasp the enormity
of the One Divine Message,

that forever has been given
to each nation, throughout all
lands and times.

Before advancement of communication
a Message yet arrived, through Messengers
that looked like their people,

in the language of each society,
with images familiar to all.

It is a simple Message, of Love and of Truth
that all were asked to follow—

Love one another.
Do unto others as you would have
Others do unto you.

Do Justice.

Respect and care for the Earth.
And daily give thanks, to the Creator of All.

One Message that echos in all hearts.
One code of honor, given to all.

May the Divine Message of Love and
Harmony lead our Spirits and hearts
to unite in peace.

And may we awaken and follow this Call,
from the Creator of All.

The Soul Is Forever Pure

The Soul is forever pure.
Remains unchanged, unblemished,

no matter what occurs
during one's lifetime.

In this sense we may understand,
that all experiences are as a dream
before the Soul—

Each one gathers and expresses
upon the manifestation,

qualities that create all existence,
all Karma.

And each one's experiences mirror
the existence in which they are
immersed.

Combined with personal desires,
this brings forth the many aspects
of creation—

The universe may be likened to
an ever-flowing vision-breath of
the Eternal Being,

Whose Wisdom urges us to create
not darkness—

but a world of splendor, glory,
and the fullness of Love and Compassion.

Teachings of Krishna

O Arjuna, the Supreme Self, having no beginning (no ending) and no attributes, even though it dwells in a body (as a realized Master), neither acts nor is touched by any action.*

Arjuna said: O Lord, I see in Your body All the gods and multitude of beings, All sages, celestial serpents, Lord Shiva as well as Lord Brahma seated on the lotus.

If the splendor of thousands of suns was to blaze forth all at once in the sky, even that would not resemble the splendor of that exalted being.

O Lord of the universe, I see You everywhere with infinite form, with many arms, stomachs, faces, and eyes. Neither do I see the beginning nor the middle nor the end of Your Universal Form.**

For the deliverance of the good, for the destruction of the evildoers, for the enthroning of the right, I am born from age to age.

Who sees Me everywhere and sees everything in Me, I am never lost, nor is he ever lost to Me.⁺

---

* Krishna; Chapter 13, verse 31; *The Essence of the Bhagavad Gita Explained by Paramhansa Yogananda*, Swami Kriyananda
** Chapter XI, Bhagavad Gita, "The Yoga of the Manifestation of the World Form: Srimad Bhagvad Gita, Dr. Manish Chandra Prabhakar
⁺ Bhagavad-gita As It Is, By His Divine Grace A. C. Bhaktivedanta Swami Prabhupada

Unerringly Guided Toward Perfection

The whole of humanity is unerringly guided toward perfection. This guidance happens nonstop, and one can say that our individual movements, and collective growth, neither end nor begin during any era, or lifetime:

Throughout all time, and all that occurs,
even in those things that we know arise

from humanity's twisting of the threads
of Wisdom,

we find that our errors are eventually guided
and brought to right,

as surely as a seed grows
in an ever-upward direction

unfurling its tiny spirit around
the rocks and roots it encounters,
on its way toward the Light.

So, too, the Divine Virtues
immaculately implanted in our hearts,
continue to advance our spirit,

leading and guiding our way
toward the One.

In this time-honored process,
throughout the epochs,

the All-in-All continues to move humanity
unto our fullness and perfection—

here on Earth,
and within the Holy Realms.

Love's Harvest

One becomes One with the Divine Love-Light
as much as it is possible for humans to be,

through a deep and unceasing devotion
to the Supreme Truth.

Yet for this to occur, an ever-increasing fire
must be built within one's heart,

and the fuel for this fire comes
from the depths of one's love.

When the fire in one's heart is large enough
it burns away all thoughts of darkness,

and in its glow, all false impressions
are cleansed from the Mirror of the Soul.

In prayer-full moments, one finds oneself
immersed in Golden Light,

and then one Knows—
that they have been held, unknowingly,

that they have been sought, by an abiding patience
and a Sacred Love, inherent in all Being.

And, in this boundless awareness,
one's heart over flows, with a gratitude

that thoroughly removes

the last traces
of one's dissolving veils.

Our Trials

The Beloved Warriors of the Most High must become adept swimmers in the whole of the ocean. Their tests are great; their lives and journeys an open book. All witness their purification, and their trials by fire.

We are shown the tremendous difficulties the Masters, Saints and Prophets of each Sacred path have had to endure, as they were becoming great leaders of their people. We are then shown their life purpose, and their experiences with the Most High. Mostly we tend to forget their enormous difficulties and trials, or to minimize them, as we become blinded by their Light. Yet, their rites of passage are not a footnote to their success, but an integral part of what made these Lovers of Truth change from the ordinary people they were, into the Divine Beings they became—

Siddhartha, the Buddha, went into the world
and experienced the suffering of the common
people, as he wandered for a time alone.

Abraham was tried by fire—tested
with the willing sacrifice of his son, Isaac.

Sarah, whose name was first Yiscah, Seer, and then Sarai, One
Who Commands, was Priestess to the Goddess,
yet according to her destiny she became a wife to Abraham, as
the world she knew disappeared.

Moses struggled with who and what he was:
leaving his high rank as Pharaoh's son,
he experienced the lowest place in his world.

Jesus had to sacrifice his own life for his Calling.

The Dalai Lama, Thich Nhat Hanh, Mother Teresa,
and many other Saints and Prophets, yielded their place of comfort,
became stripped to their foundations, before attaining
their zeniths.

For the darkness exists
and the Light exists,

and all must pass through trials of darkness on
their way to the Light.

And though they be great or small, our
difficulties become the foundation upon which
all must climb,

in order to attain Union, with the
Most Supreme.

The One Being One

The uncountable names of the Most Supreme, the Most High, the Unlimited, represent the multitude of innumerable facets and Divine qualities, of the Creator of All.

These are just a few of the thousands of names that are being used, and have been used throughout the world, in all societies, in every Epoch, to honor the All-In-All. Yet even if they were combined, all sacred names could never restrict, or hope to define, the magnificence of the Most Exalted. Nor can any of these glorious names circumscribe, or in any way limit, the Boundless One, the Ever Living, the Bestower of Light, the Most Compassionate, the Merciful, the Determiner of Life and Death.

For the Fashioner of All has made it absolutely clear, that there is no single name able to completely hold, convey or carry—

The Source of All
The Holy One
The Father, The Mother
The Originator
The Omniciscient
The One Deserving All Praise

For every breath of every being,
every movement, of every atom,
in the outer and the Inner Realms,
are only a reflection of:

The One Being One
The Comforter
The Divine Essence
The Alpha and Omega.

And each and every flower petal
and each and every star,
and each tear, on the face
of every one

are all singing the heart songs of—

"I WILL BE WHAT I SHALL BE" *

---

* Exodus 3:13-15, Hebrew, The Most High answered Moses when he asked what is His name was, "Ehyeh Asher Ehyeh", Translation by Rashi, from Hertz, p. 215

Unstoppable, the Holy River

Water arrives from the sky, freezes and melts, flows around all obstacles, or sinks beneath the Earth's surface if there is an opening through which it may pass.

Like this the Holy Message of the Most High mightily bursts forth from the depths or the heights of life when need is high, and sinks below the surface into hidden places, as the times ordain:

Unstoppable, the Holy River,
the Message of our Union
with the All-In-All,

unceasingly flows
through the Epochs.

Encircling the Earth with Love and Light, the
Eternal Well-Spring of Wisdom and Truth

wanders
as a Sacred Caravan,

gathering and disbursing its
Life-Giving sweetness

unto all who happen
to stumble upon it,
as the world turns.

Your Beauty Eyes Are Needed

As we remove the coverings of our limited personality and reveal our Inner Light, we find ourselves becoming softer and more open-hearted. Throughout our days, we feel more loving, compassionate and present. Dedicating our lives to a path of peace, we can sense ourselves moving ever closer to the Most High, whose Love we perceive filling our lives more and more—"As in Heaven, so on Earth."

Here is a meditation to help those of us who are struggling to evolve into our fullness of Love and Harmony. It may be spoken walking out of doors, or if sitting quietly in our room, we can simply practice following our breath in and out, as outlined here:

Walking or Sitting Practice—

20

Take an even number of steps while inhaling, matching the rhythm of the words to your gait, and for the same number of steps exhale, while saying the words. Repeat each word softly or silently as you take each step.

If sitting simply say aloud or silently each word, in a comfortable rhythm per inhale and exhale. Your breath should be very easy:

With-in all things
All Ways, all forms

Ex-ists the One
Who formed All Ways

I sit with Thee
I walk with Thee

I sit with Thee
I walk with Thee

Repeat the last four lines over and over as you walk or sit, as many times as you like, keeping the words in rhythm with your breath. Gently observe or imagine the colors and sounds of the insects, flowers and trees, the plants and the birds, the sky and the light surrounding you, as you breathe in, and then consciously return all of these essences that you have received on the inhale, placing them upon your exhale. If sitting inside, close your eyes and imagine distant mountains, and try to feel your breath touching the trees, the streams, and the flowers, and returning to you. In both cases experience Nature as pleased by your gift and attention.

Walking or sitting: Let the pores of your skin open and breathe with your breath, in and out. Imagine the flowers and trees receiving and breathing in your exhaled gift, as you receive, in turn, their gifts on your inhale. Your sense of Presence and vitality will increase over time. Note how you feel at the beginning and at the ending of your practice.

Crosses All Borders

The Most Supreme exists for most of us within the realm of philosophy: one has an idea of a Creator-of-All, and yet has no direct experience of its substantive reality. Yet, if we add to the 'The Divine One,' the words, 'is Love,' then we are on to something we can begin to grasp: for we all know what Love is, and what Love is not:

All who choose to walk the Honor-bound High-Ways of Love
discover them to be well traveled—

Walking with Sincerity upon one's path one finds
the 'Creator of All' crosses all borders, enters all
nations, and yes, there is Love.

Peering into the hearts of children, women and men,
one finds that yes, there is Love.

Within the hearts of animals, fish, and even birds —
once again one finds, that yes, there is Love.

Seeing a flower tenderly offering her beauty
to all who pass her way; marveling at the Earth,

Her bounty that endures our many mistakes,
one finds that yes, there is Love.

Delving into the hearts of the most troubled
the murderers and rapists,

one finds a broken heart and mind,

only needing to remember—
that yes, there is Love.

Finally one finds no tongue that moves,
no living cell that does not carry
deep within itself,

the Divine Essence of Love.

And should the seeker continue to
walk the honor-bound High-Ways of

Love, one day at the fountainhead,
in gratitude they exclaim—

"Oh yes! Here is Love!"

The Alpha and the Omega

Neither darkness nor Light can exist separately from the One and the Only. Both belong to, are integral to, the foundational nature of the Most Supreme—the Alpha and Omega.

The cyclical rise and fall of human societies,
including all nations, people,

and the entirety of Nature is Known,
as all things are Known, by the All-in-All—

From the beginning of beginnings
unto the utmost future,

our journey on Earth includes
the darkness and the Light.

Both have equally served to advance
our collective development,
since existence began.

Yet just as perennial flowers arrive in Spring,
offering their sweet colors and fragrances,
only to wither and die each year—

so too, the generations of humanity
rise and fall

until they return once more
into the quietness from whence they have come.

Then the Earth reshapes and renews Herself,
and the Epoch of Peace,
ever desired and predicted

is born anew

in the never-ending,
ever beginning,

Circle of Life.

Teachings of Thich Nhat Hanh

We have the seeds, the potential, in us for understanding, love, compassion, and insight, as well as the seeds of anger, hate, and greed.

While we can't avoid all the suffering in life, we can suffer much less by not watering the seeds of suffering inside us.

There is no need to try to be something else. We only need to let ourselves be what we already are, and enjoy ourselves just as we are. That feeling, that realization, is our true home. Each of us has a true home inside.

My actions are my only true belongings. I cannot escape the consequences of my actions. My actions are the ground upon which I stand.

The quality of our life depends on the quality of the seeds that lie deep in our consciousness.

If we are peaceful, if we are happy, we can blossom like a flower, and everyone in our entire society will benefit from our peace.*

---

* Quotes from Thich Nhat Hanh, see copyright page for permissions and sources

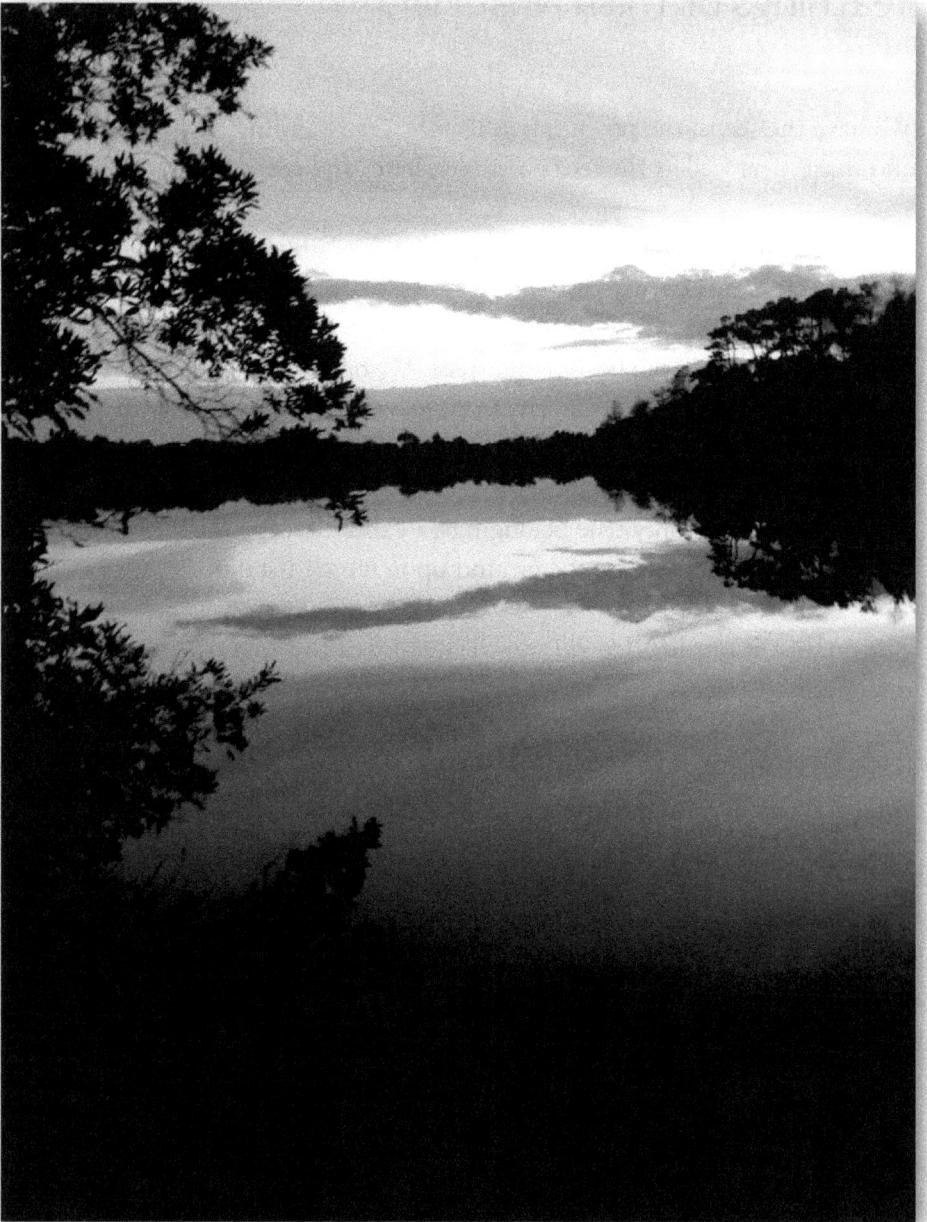

When the Heart Becomes Open In Prayer

All prayers which are heart filled, emerge and arrive on wings of Light, into the Holy Realms, and the Ears of the Most High.

During unobstructed Prayer-Union,
with-in the Supreme dimension of Love and Light,

Divine Blessings are showered
upon the pure of heart.

Yet the moment one's mind,
responding from a limited perspective
and filled with worldly knowledge,

begins to analyze the gift…

the translucent, shimmering state
of Holiness disappears—

retracts behind the vibrational curtain
of the physical reality,

that forever separates this Earthly Realm,
from the Eternal Garden
of Beauty, Truth, and Love.

Love Is One With Truth

When deep feelings of True Love permeate our Heart-Being, we can say that we are leaving the world of variety, and entering into Union with the Most High.

A question may arise: "What is True Love?" An answer bubbles forth, "Everyone knows what True Love is." Yet we may have forgotten, that the highest form of love is Truth itself:

At any moment, in the twinkling of an eye,
whenever Love is present, Truth is also there—

True Love is found in moments of perfect beauty,
in complete surrender to joy.

True Love is found in tender intimacy,
when all traces of longing recede from view.

It is True Love that carries each Soul
to Earth, to live in a physical body.

And, at the moment of death,
the combined forces of Love and Truth

gain one sanction
to the Holy Realms.

Louder Than Words

We have not been taught from our youth how to keep our minds still.

From morning unto evening, from childhood to death,
every moment the mind is filled with words:
things we are thinking of doing
things we have already done, and things yet to come.

When our mind is full of chatter, our attention is diverted
and our eyes cannot harmonize with, or reflect to others,
the fullness of life occurring this moment.

Imagine how beautiful our time on Earth would be,
if we were attentively present to the incredible beauty
in our lives. How many lovely images we would capture
and remember at the end of this life—

Some perhaps as these:

Sunlight, shining on the petals of sweet-scented lilacs,
dancing in a lovely spring breeze, as we stroll through
our garden.

The shifting colors and shapes
of white, fluffy clouds, floating softly
across the sky, on a glorious summer day.

The beauty of our friend's hand
resting on our table, as we share
our evening meal.

Our beloved's peaceful smile,
their eyes softly meeting ours
after tender lovemaking.

Our pet, running to greet us
with exuberant joy—ears flying,
eyes bright, as we arrive home
at the end of our day.

When the mind and body are calm,
the entire being is as clear
as an undisturbed lake—

able to reflect,
and perfectly harmonize

with the offerings on
our table of Life.

Then, oh then, the eyes will
begin to speak,
louder than any words.

In the Center of a Holy Pearl

Walking in the center of a Holy Pearl one
comes to understand,

that the sole purpose of
Highways of Wisdom and Truth,

are to bring forth enormous Love-Light
and Life,

for the benefit of the whole
world.

Beloved one,

don't settle

for anything

less.

Your Journey to Truth Begins Here

Remaining untaught from our youth
about the one life we all share,

We feel that the lives that we harm
or we kill

Are not part of our own sacred flesh.

O please hear the cries from the
oceans, and listen to voices in pain—

Calling to us from the trees and the hills,
from the fields and the mountains and plains.

Try to remember the beings,
that give you your meat every day.

See their dear eyes, and their innocence,
please raise them in honor, not shame.

Take a walk in the meadows and valleys,
spend a day with the flowers and deer,

Open your hearts, and feel what is real,
your journey to Truth begins here.

Our Only Task

Seek to Live your life in an Open-Hearted state of Being—
Entering every moment fully awake, into the Sacredness
of a Love-Full Reality:

It only takes a moment to remember,
the heart feelings, the bright colors and
soft sounds,

the sweet fragrances, and the Luminous Light —
that blesses the whole of our being

whenever we experience
an Awakened State of Love.

Remembering these times,
moments we felt that holiness was indeed
present on Earth we begin to understand,

that the only task humanity
has ever been asked 'To Do' —

individually, or collectively,
throughout the All-Ways

is to experience the Divine Presence to
daily Witness the Sacredness of life,

so that one day we may

become—

Only Love.

(We really do have it in us)

Every Single Morning

Every single morning
without fail

the Natural world awakens to
celebrate the dawn.

Exactly what are you allowing
to interfere

with taking the time to praise
this amazing world

at the birthing of each
new day?

Our Union With Purity

The Innermost state of 'Union with Purity' is available to all of humanity, regardless of country, ideology, or religious choice. We all know this is our commonality—the ground wherein all differences cease between the members of our world family:

Our Union with Purity is an experience
no carnival ride can match.

How could anyone be satisfied
with what humanity has created
for pastimes

if they have once experienced:

The sounds of a bubbling brook as
it rushes along

through sun and through shadow
in a dappled-green forest,

while we stand—watching and waiting,
all senses alert, hoping only for

a chance to spy—
dashing along the clear, rocky bottom

the quick, freedom flight
of a red-spotted trout as it

swiftly swishes past, with
no care in the world—

for anything.

And, at the instant we see
her all thoughts fly away—

and the presence of awe becomes all
that we know—
of life.

Lady Wisdom

Does not Wisdom call,
    And understanding lift up Her voice?
On top of the heights beside the way,
    Where the paths meet, She takes Her stand;
Beside the gates, at the opening to the city,
    At the entrance of the doors, She cries out:
"To you, O men, I call,
    And My voice is to the sons and daughters of men.
"O naive ones, understand prudence;
    And, O fools, understand Wisdom.
"Listen, for I will speak noble things;
    And the opening of My lips *will reveal* right things.
"For My mouth will utter truth;
    And wickedness is an abomination to My lips.
"All the utterances of My mouth are in righteousness;
    There is nothing crooked or perverted in them.
"They are all straightforward to those who understand,
    And right to those who find knowledge.
"Take My instruction and not silver,
    And knowledge rather than choicest gold.
"For Wisdom is better than jewels;
    And all desirable things cannot compare with Her.
"I, Wisdom, dwell with prudence,
    And I find knowledge *and* discretion.
"The Way of the Most High is to hate evil;
    Pride and arrogance and the evil way
    And the perverted mouth, I hate.
"Counsel is Mine and sound Wisdom;
    I am understanding, power is Mine.

By Me reign all who judge rightly.
"I love those who love Me;
    And those who diligently seek Me will find Me.
"Riches and honor are with Me,
    Enduring wealth and righteousness.
"My fruit is better than gold, even pure gold,
    And My yield *better* than choicest silver.
"I walk in the way of righteousness,
    In the midst of the paths of justice,
To endow those who love Me with wealth,
    That I may fill their treasuries.
"The One possessed Me at the beginning of this Way,
    Before all works of old.
"From everlasting I was established,
    From the beginning, from the earliest times of the Earth.
"When there were no depths I was brought forth,
    When there were no springs abounding with water.
"Before the mountains were settled,
    Before the hills I was brought forth;
While the Divine had not yet made the Earth and the fields,
    Nor the first dust of the world.
"When the Most High established the heavens, I was there,
    When the Most Supreme inscribed a circle on the face of the deep,
When the Divine made firm the skies above,
    When the springs of the deep became fixed,
When the Eternal set for the sea its boundary
    So that the water would not transgress the Supreme command,
    When the Most High marked out the foundations of the Earth;
Then I was there *as* a Master Creator;
    And I was daily *a* delight,
    Rejoicing always with the Divine,
Rejoicing in the world, the Earth,
    And *having* my delight in the children of on Earth.

"Now therefore, *O* sons and daughters, listen to Me,
    For blessed are they who keep My ways.
"Heed instruction and be wise,
    And do not neglect *it.*
"Blessed are those who listen to Me,
    Watching daily at My gates,
    Waiting at My doorposts.
"For they who find Me find life
    And obtain favor from the Most High.
"But they who go against Wisdom injure themselves;
    And all those who hate Wisdom love death."*

---

* Proverbs 8:1 – 8:23

One Creator, One Breath

Even though we may desire, or claim ownership of portions of Earth, absolute ownership, and a clear title, always remain in the Hands of the Most High.

Today not only portions of the Earth, but water, plants, animals, and even tiny cells may be bought and sold, patented and privately owned. Yet, there is one thing that belongs to all beings equally: One thing that everyone freely takes, and freely gives to others—our breath—

Our breath we cannot live without,
breath we take, breath we give—

freely received, freely returned,
all day, and all night long,

all Being, all life breathes.

And all who draw breath
never think of keeping it

hold no thought of hoarding it,

feel no Inner urge to grab
another's share—

but simply enjoy the Gift.

For we all know without a doubt
that the air we breathe belongs,

as the whole Earth in truth belongs—
not to us

but the Source of All, the All-in-All,
Who eternally creates this Earth

and the Universe,
and all who draw breath therein.

This Is the Plan

One begins the journey believing they want to find the Source of All: This is the plan.

At the start of one's journey to the Most High, one believes the Divine exists 'somewhere' outside of us. All of the meditations, prayers, chants and studies, on the religious and spiritual paths throughout the world, are seen as aids in this honorable search: "I am here; Divinity is there."

Along one's chosen path one often finds that the more they practice, the more 'other centered' they become. Some seekers may even experience a Union with the Beloved: During prayer or meditation, or during moments of Inspiration, breathing One Breath—as a newborn, whose umbilical cord still pulses for a few final moments, before separation from its mother occurs. Like this, as one returns to everyday awareness, it is possible to Remember the place where one was One, and not two:

After a time of rapture
one emerges—

aware yet of 'That Perfection'
right in the place where one is standing…
or kneeling.

Over-flowing with Great Love
one may venture to implore—

"O where do I end, Beloved One
and where dost thou begin?"

Dear ones—for those who have been 'here'
and those who have not,

I pray you will forgive this traveler
an impossible task—

to even attempt to write
anything at all

of a portal
existing beyond time—

is nothing short of pure folly.

Teachings of Hafiz

Awake Awhile

Awake awhile.
It does not have to be Forever,
Right now.
One step upon the Sky's soft skirt
Would be enough.
Hafiz,
Awake awhile.
Just one True moment of Love
Will last for days.
Rest all your elaborate plans and tactics
For Knowing Him,
For they are all just frozen spring buds
Far,
So far from Summer's Divine Gold.
Awake, my dear.
Be kind to your sleeping heart.
Take it out into the vast fields of Light
And let it breathe.
Say,
"Love,
Give me back my wings. Lift me,
Lift me nearer."
Say to the sun and moon,
Say to our dear Friend,
"I will take You up now, Beloved,
On that wonderful
Dance You promised!"

We Should Talk About This Problem

There is a Beautiful Creature
Living in a hole you have dug.

So at night
I set fruit and grains
And little pots of wine and milk
Beside your soft earthen mounds,

And I often sing.

But still, my dear,
You do not come out.

I have fallen in love with Someone
Who hides inside you.

We should talk about this problem—

Otherwise,
I will never leave you alone.

A Divine Invitation

You have been invited to meet
The Friend
No one can resist a Divine invitation.
That narrows down all our choices
To just two:
We can come to God
Dressed for Dancing,

Or
Be carried on a stretcher
To God's Ward.

~~~~~~~~~~~~~~~~~~~~~~~

Would You Think It Odd?

Would you think it odd if Hafiz said,

"I am in love with every church
And mosque
And temple
And any kind of shrine

Because I know it is there
That people say the different names
Of the One God."

Would you tell your friends
I was a bit strange if I admitted

I am indeed in love with every mind
And heart and body.

O I am sincerely
Plumb crazy
About your every thought and yearning
And limb

Because, my dear,
I know
That it is through these

That you search for Him.*

_____

* Hafiz Poems, by Daniel Ladinsky, see copyright page for permissions and sources

Our Own Hearts and Hands

If there is ever a moment one feels that an 'other'
is in need of a swift application of hard-heartedness
in order to show them the way,

in that moment one is really standing beneath
the other,

trapped within the limited viewpoint
of an individuated mind.

If at all possible in these intense times,
before losing ground and becoming hurtful,
briefly pause and consider:

that the 'other' has arrived at the
place they are standing

because their spirit has already
been broken—

by a too harsh world.

This small seed of thought-fullness,
will yield a field filled with mercy
and compassion,

instead of dislike, disrespect
and disregard.

And, rather than seeking to bring the other down
through harsh words or measures,

in this clear reflection, all desire for
hot-blooded action is transformed,
into a healing balm one knows

is to be applied—
by none 'other' than ourselves.

And if our angry head can follow
the Wisdom of our heart,

we will find we are being moved
from within—to become

not an executioner,

but the heart, and the hands,
of a true friend.

O Let the Women Stand!

O let the women stand!
Let them rise to their absolute fullness.

Let them birth their precious gifts of
Love and blessings on Earth.

O let the men honor the gifts
that women long to shower

upon our broken Earth...
and their dear ones.

O let the women rise!
Let them waken and rise!

O let the women stand!

Guidance Arrives

Humanity is climbing as one family, upward and toward the Light—
moving with certainty, and unerring Guidance:

War, killing and oppression of all kinds
create a rebounding movement

within the hearts of all who are called upon
to partake, or witness horrific deeds.

And yet all sides—the oppressors and responders,
as well as the victims,

are breathing each breath from the One Creation
for there is nowhere else to be:

During times of unwanted surrender,
Guidance often arrives

urging us to 'Do Something'—

to root out the evil, to bring forth,
in the midst of chaos and despair,

some offering of Truth, and Love.

This Inner desire to 'Do'
is a response from the Most High,

Who constantly Guides all Being,
from deep inside,

all who cry out in prayer.

The Heart of a Holy Sage

The heart of a Holy Sage is attuned to the hearts and minds of all beings, not only to those on their particular Way.

The very being and essence of a Holy Sage is all Love and all peace. When we are in their presence, everyone, from the vast variety of paths and streams, experiences the Wisdom and Grace of the One Source of All—

Rising from our limited views, we come to see, that the Most High exists with-in each and every pure religious and Spiritual path. Though the priest or monk, master, rabbi or imam, may speak to those present about the Divine One, the Great Spirit, Jesus or Buddha, Krishna or Hashem, Mohammed or the Holy Mother, if we have the desire to open our hearts, all become immersed, in the Holiness present at that time.

We might understand this better if we think about those who journeyed to India, from all faith traditions, to visit Mother Teresa. Though we know that each path holds different ideologies about the All-in-All, we still hear stories about the Presence of Holiness experienced by those who met Mother Teresa, regardless of their religious stream. And even when many hundreds or thousands were with her, people felt they were sharing *the same experience of Holiness* as everyone who was there.

This feeling of Sacredness has also occurred for those who have been in the Presence of the Dali Lama, Thich Nhat Hahn, Amma-Ji, Yogananda, Meher Baba, Wallace Black Elk, and many other advanced Spiritual Beings: their Presence enlivens and awakens our own connections with the Divine.

In fact, experiences of Divinity are so extraordinary, that when we are gathered around a Holy Master, Saint or Sage, collective moments of holiness and union transport us all into a state of bliss, wonder and awe:

In the Presence of a Holy Sage
all sense of fighting fades;

all inharmonious desires evaporate,
as mist rising in the morning sun.

All doubt, all feelings of contention,
all thoughts of dissension on
any point at all—pass from sight,

'til all that is left in our tender, opened hearts
is a warm and shining Love-Light,

a feeling that Heavenly life
has been brought to Earth

and to us—

through the Awakened Heart, of a Beloved
'Warrior of Truth.'

And all of this occurs with no words—
there is no need for translation

because our gift arrives as we simply breathe,
in peaceful silence,

amidst the radiating Peace
and Grace,

that surrounds, and emanates
from the Heart, of a Holy
Sage.

Teachings of Mother Teresa

If we have no peace, it is because we have forgotten that we belong to each other.

Do not wait for leaders; do it alone, person to person.

Everybody today seems to be in such a terrible rush, anxious for greater developments and greater riches and so on, so that children have very little time for their parents. Parents have very little time for each other, and in the home begins the disruption of peace of the world.

I want you to be concerned about your next door neighbor.
Do you know your next door neighbor?

It is not the magnitude of our actions but the amount of love that is put into them that matters.

We think sometimes that poverty is only being hungry, naked and homeless. The poverty of being unwanted, unloved and uncared for is the greatest poverty. We must start in our own homes to remedy this kind of poverty.

Spread love everywhere you go. Let no one ever come to you without leaving happier.

Intense love does not measure, it just gives.

---

* Quotes from Mother Teresa, see copyright page for permission and sources

Winning the Sacred Gift of Life

Are blows really necessary to open our hearts to Love?

Have you ever seen the faces of venerated elders, the women
and the men of the ancient Walks? If you have ever seen their faces,
you will have your answer:

Lined and worn through many battles,
the faces of elders contain impressions of the
pains and sorrows they have endured.

Yet just look in their eyes:

If they shine, with the radiant glow
of Love-Light,

and if within their smile and glance
you feel a deep sense of welcome,

and see a reflection of the strength
and depth of Wisdom and Love,

that offers a sweet tenderness
to all who come their way—

you will understand that they have won
the Sacred Gift of Life:

What was lost was their ego; what
was gained was the Love of the
One Heart of All.

During Prayer

During the heart of one's prayer,
standing in Blissful Union,

in the ever-growing, softly-glowing
warmth and Blessings of Divine Light,

All that is Present is—

ONE Breathing

ONE Being

ONE Loving

ONE.

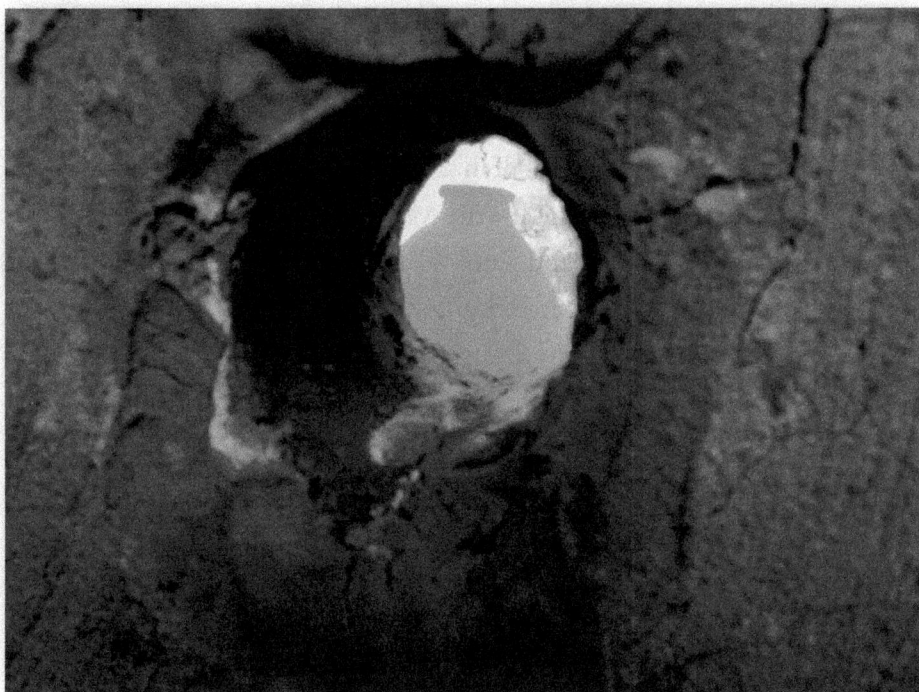

The Cooking Pot

Slowly, humanity is coming to a boil; bubbles of Living Wisdom arrive at the surface, and the One stirring the Cooking Pot sings the ancient Blessing Song: "It is Good, it is Good."

The Holy Mothers, the great teachers of humanity, including the Goddesses Anna, Alat, Elat, Ima, Innana, Tara, Asherah, Ashtarte, Ellah, Aloah, Radha, Parvati, Mahadevi, Kali, Pele, Quan Yin, Isis, Hathor, Ma'at, and more—for more than 35,000 years, carried and offered Divine Wisdom —and the Epoch of the Mother as Goddess was upon the Earth, and the fires began to warm the water in the Cooking Pot.

Then the Holy Fathers, the great teachers of humanity, mingled with the Holy Mothers, including: Maya Mae Thorani and Buddha, Yazata and Zoroaster, Eloah and El, Radha and Krishna, Parvati and Shiva, Yiscah Sarai Sarah and Abrahm Abraham, Ziporah and Moses, Miriam and Caleb, Elisheba and Aaron, Rachel and Jacob, Mary the Magdala and Jesus, Khadija and Mohammed, Spider Woman and Tawa, Haumea and Sky Father, Izanami and Izanagi—and the Epoch of the Father as Creator was birthing upon the Earth, and the water began to simmer in the Cooking Pot.

In these Sacred Ways, on Eternal Paths,
the Great Teachers of humanity walk.

And wherever and whenever their Truth is brought forth,
those who are chosen, who can See and can Hear—
are often persecuted, or killed.

The world is on its perfect course: there is no hurrying
it along. Step by step, in absolute time, Teachers arrive
as bubbles of Holy Love and Light,

and, in their bursting, they shower the whole Being, with
sweet drops of Wisdom and Blessing.

And as we can Know, and as we can feel,
the waters in the Cooking Pot are coming to boil.

And all the while the Supreme One continues
to stir, and to sing the ancient Blessing Song:

"It is Good, it is Good."

Virtue and Personal Quests

What use the ancient admonition, "Honor all harm none?"

Whenever our movements cause harm
no matter how virtuous the claim,

we are bound to fall short
and to miss our aim. For it

is not the brief success that
matters, in the long haul,

but to complete the primal purpose
for which we have come:

To succeed in fulfilling
our highest goal, our movements

must be Honor-bound
all along our way.

And, until all beings are Seen, and Known
as the Most High,

and treated as such—

we have not yet arrived
at our Highest Ideal,

the Virtue
of the Masters and Saints.

Teachings of Avatar Meher Baba

Law is good. This universe is based on the divine law of good which pervades all existence.

The Avatar is always one and the same, because God is always One and the Same, the Eternal, Indivisible, Infinite One, who manifests Himself in the form of man as the Avatar, as the Messiah, as the Prophet, as the Ancient One—the Highest of the High. This Eternally One and the Same Avatar repeats His manifestation from time to time, in different cycles, adopting different human forms and different names, in different places, to reveal Truth in different garbs and different languages, in order to raise humanity from the pit of ignorance and help free it from the bondage of delusions.

Shun those Masters who are like multicolored electric signs that flash on and off, brightening the dark sky of your world and leaving you in darkness again.

Being good is a good binding. You must either be good or bad. Bad is like bound wrists. Good is like bound feet. Kabir writes beautifully about this: "Good keeps your hands free, so that you can even unbind your feet. Be good. It pays. Bad makes you mad (insane). Good takes you to God. And the best way to become good is to serve others and try to make others happy.

Everyone, no matter how depraved, can gradually become better and better until he becomes the best example for all mankind. There is always hope for everyone; none is utterly lost, and none need despair. It remains true, however, that the way to divinity lies through the renunciation of evil in favor of good.

All of this world's confusion and chaos was inevitable and no one is to blame. What had to happen has happened; and what has to happen will happen. There was and is no way out except through my coming in your midst. I had to come, and I have come. I am the Ancient One.[*]

Living Far Removed From Nature

How have we become separated from the conscious awareness of the very Life that flows through our Being? Withdrawing ourselves far from the Natural World, this is what has happened—

> Living removed as we are, from the daily experiences of heart opening, that automatically occur within our body, mind and spirit, whenever we are in Nature's Presence, has led us to believe that we are separate from the world that surrounds us, and the Holy Source of All.

Long ago people lived and breathed as One Being within the very heart of Nature's life. They experienced Her beauty and Her power, each day of their lives. With such deep and personal contact, the Divine Essence of the Source of Life was Known, honored and enjoyed, and ever-present on Earth.

Thus it did not take much training for their little ones to begin to understand—that the life they saw reflected in the eyes of the eagle or the lion, the bear or the deer, was as vital and Wisdom-full as the life they saw reflected in the eyes of their own dear family.

Their children were lovingly taught that each being carries a different reflection of the Inner Wisdom and Power that arrives from the One Source: One bird can see from great heights, and plot and instant kill, while another has eyes that hold no such intention of harm.

In this way it became clear, through daily immersion in the Natural world, that the Inner, Living-Light that enabled each Being to have their own, unique capacity, was the same as the Inner, Living- Light that beamed through their own eyes. And it is this direct, personal experience, of the One Source that flows through all creatures, all existence, that is in such great lack and need today.

Realizing Our Oneness

The yearning, and the goal of life, is to be completely whole…and to do this we must realize our oneness with the Omnipresent Divinity.

It happens—
while one is completely at ease and forgets themselves,
amidst a quiet ocean sunrise;

It occurs—
while one is lost inside the silence
of softly falling snow.

At these out-of-time moments
it often happens—

that all at once, the everyday mind-world
intrudes—comes lapping on the shores of
our heart, and causes us to sigh:

"O Beloved! Why such confusion?

O Divine One! Why all the greed and war?

When this blessed Joy is available
to all Lovers,

exists in every heart,
and the smallest opening into Love

can usher us to a place of
peace on Earth?"

A quiet voice gently implores:

"O Beloved, please don't wander!

Dearest One, stay awhile longer
in the Garden of Beauty.

O, please, Dear Heart stay—

if you can…

Enjoy this Sacred Gift!"

Teachings of Buddha

Radiate boundless love towards the entire world.[1]

Just as a mother would protect her only child with her life, even so let one cultivate a boundless love towards all beings.[2]

Whatever is not yours: let go of it. Your letting go of it will be for your long-term happiness and benefit.[3]

Whatever has the nature of arising has the nature of ceasing.[4]

Understanding is the heartwood of well-spoken words.[5]

Should a seeker not find a companion who is better or equal, let them resolutely pursue a solitary course. [6]

Ceasing to do evil, Cultivating the good, Purifying the heart: This is the teaching of the Buddhas.[7]

They blame those who remain silent, they blame those who speak much, they blame those who speak in moderation. There is none in the world who is not blamed. [8]

May all beings have happy minds.[9]

[1,2] Karaniya Metta Sutta
[3] Na Tumhaka of the Samyutta Nikaya
[4] Kimsuka Sutta
[5] Kimsila Sutta
[6] Dhammapada, Verse 61
[7] Dhammapada, Verse 183
[8] Dhammapada, Verse 227
[9] Karaniya Metta Sutta

If a man going down into a river, swollen and swiftly flowing, is carried away by the current — how can he help others across?[10]

The calmed say that what is well-spoken is best; second, that one should say what is right, not unrighteous; third, what's pleasing, not displeasing; fourth, what is true, not false. [11]

Resolutely train yourself to attain peace[12]

All tremble at violence, all fear death. Putting oneself in the place of another, one should not kill nor cause another to kill.[13]

[10, 11] Nipata Sutta
[12] Utthana Sutta of the Sutta Nipata
[13] Dhammapada, Verse

Until the Circle Is Whole

Humanity stands between the Divine and the manifest, and through the Human Spiritual Capacity, all planes of existence may be realized.

The destination of each Soul is to realize, while in individuated Human form, its Union with the Divine. This includes the complete awareness, and actualization, of our human Spiritual Capacity.

Ancient civilizations did not have detailed knowledge of the physical realm. Instead of Scientific knowledge, it's gift to us was the opening of humanities awareness of the Spiritual Realm.

And although those living during this earliest epoch were poor in physical comforts, they experienced the richness of the Spiritual, Inner Realms.

For example, in ancient times both the human body and the body of the Earth were considered to be holy, were seen as living expressions of the Most High. In contrast in our modern epoch, without a conscious awareness of, or belief in, our ever-present Union with the Most Supreme, our physical bodies and the body of the Earth are easily abused, and thoughtlessly desecrated.

Today humanity is arriving at the birthing time of a new epoch and many Souls are beginning to open the door of their heart, just as a waking flower arises from its deep, winter slumber. And, as the first rays of the morning sun touch our Inner Being, a silent but pervasive Presence emerges on the horizon of our awareness—Calling us to Awaken! Urging us to respond:

From a place of softening and opening our Hearts,
we come to realize,

that there has been an over-arching theme
guiding humanity's long, collective growth:

Each Soul is an integral part
of the whole Living Being—

and each, in their own Way, advances
toward the Supreme Glor y,

grows into their fullness
of Love and Light and Divinity,
as the Circle waxes whole.

Teachings of Kabir

How Humble Is God

God is the tree in the forests that
allows itself to die and will not defend itself in front of those
with the ax, not wanting to cause them
shame.

And God is the Earth that will allow itself to
be deformed by man's tools, but He cries; yes, God cries,
but only in front of His closest ones.

And a beautiful animal is being beaten to death,
but nothing can make God break His silence
to the masses
and say,

"Stop, please stop, why are you doing this
to Me?"

How humble is God?
Kabir wept
when I
knew.*

---

*How Humble Is God by Daniel Ladinsky, see copyright page for permission and source

High-Ways of Love and Light and Life

The longing,
the emptiness we feel deep inside,

the hunger we try to fill
with the "things" of our lives

can never be fully sated
until we have realized our Oneness,

with the Source of Life
from whence we have come.

Of course this Holy Communion is possible
while we yet walk this Earth—

for the Great Ones have established
the Inner Path-Ways,

inviting all to witness,
in advance,

where they will one day reside
as welcome guests

in the Supreme Realms.

Awakened Hearts Understand

Where do all of the goddesses and gods come from? And what do they rely on upon for their source of strength?

Gods and goddesses, throughout the ages, have a divine father and mother from whom they have taken birth. And if their divine parents have names, they will speak of their parents, and their parent's parents, who were also gods or goddesses.

This naming of each one's ancestors continues until finally, the Most Ancient One, the Source of All, becomes symbolized—sometimes as the Sun, the Moon, the Nameless, the Formless, the Creator of All.

And from the most ancient of days unto today, no matter the epoch or name, all beloved goddesses and gods ultimately perform the same function for humanity: that of awakening Divine Love, Truth and Justice, as they continue to provide the examples of what it means to be fully human:

All humanity with Awakened Hearts
understand

that Divine Love and Truth
are the powers

that run
the whole S/He-bang:

They are the only goal—

All there is to be,
All there is to become.

Teachings of Native Americans

All the stones that are around here, each one has a language of its own. Even the Earth has a song.
> — Wallace Black Elk, Lakota Sioux

The aquifers breathe in rain and snow and breathe it out. The springs are the breathing holes. Humankind is a participant in water-life. Mankind's thoughts influence whether the rain and snow comes"
> — Hopi Elder Vernon Masayesva.

There can never be peace between nations until there is first known that true peace which is within the Souls of men.
> — Grandfather Black Elk, Lakota Sioux

With Beauty before me, may I walk.
With Beauty behind me, may I walk.
With Beauty above me, may I walk.
With Beauty below me, may I walk.
With Beauty all around me, may I walk.
> — Navajo Prayer

I salute the light within your eyes where the whole universe dwells. For when you are at that center within you and I am that place within me, we shall be as one."
> — Crazy Horse, Lakota Sioux

Hold on to what is good,
even if it is a handful of Earth.

Hold on to what you believe,
even if it is a tree that stands by itself.

Hold onto what you must do,
even if it is a long way from here.

Hold onto your life,
even if it is easier to let go.

Hold onto my hand, even if
someday I'll be gone away.

– A Pueblo Native American Prayer

"The Great Spirit has taught you and us both one thing- that we should love one another and fear him. He has taught us by his Spirit, and white men by the Good Book, and it is all one."

– Chief Mononcue, Ohio Wendat Nation

The Eternal Wheel of Life

With an unobstructed view one can
clearly see

all Souls in motion,
each traveling within their own flock,
upon one Golden Ray

of the Grand Mandala
of the Universe.

Like this we journey with the Most Supreme,
the All-in-All,

Who, residing in the center as
a blazing Sun,

endlessly carries all Souls on
Rays of Love and Light,

as together we traverse the Empyrean
in harmony,

riding upon the Eternal Wheel
of Life.

When All Life Has Voice

Along our current path, things of the hearth
and heart are less desired, than things in the
business world.

Love for family, and care for our Earth take a back seat,
while our search for connection with the Most Supreme
comes around on weekends, if it comes around at all.

In such a world, when one's aim is
the gathering of name and fame

the River of Life flows away from
the family.

Then the killing and harming of animals,
plants and people comes easily

for our hearts have not been opened
to experience their pain.

In earlier epochs the River of Life
flowed toward the family,

Served as a constant reminder
of our Union with all,

and offered this certainty—

That each and every life is a
part of One life, One Being.

And in a world where family
and Nature are recognized
as belonging to each other,

as originating from the
same Source

all Spirits,
all Hearts are honored—

are spoken to
listened to,

and in turn,
all life has voice.

Teachings of Lao Tzu

1
*Existence is beyond the power of words
To define:
Terms may be used
But are none of them absolute.
In the beginning of heaven and earth there were no words,
Words came out of the womb of matter;
And whether a man dispassionately
Sees to the core of life
Or passionately
Sees the surface,
The core and the surface
Are essentially the same,
Words making them seem different
Only to express appearance.
If name be needed, wonder names them both:
From wonder into wonder
Existence opens.

15
*Long ago the land was ruled with a wisdom
Too fine, too deep, to be fully understood
And, since it was beyond men's full understanding,
Only some of it has come down to us, as in these sayings:
'Alert as a winter-farer on an icy stream,'
'Wary as a man in ambush,'
'Considerate as a welcome guest,"'
'Selfless as melting ice,'
'Green as an uncut tree,'

91

'Open as a valley,'
And this one also, 'Roiled as a torrent.'
Why roiled as a torrent?
Because when a man is in turmoil how shall he find peace
Save by staying patient till the stream clears?
How can a man's life keep its course
If he will not let it flow?
Those who flow as life flows know
They need no other force:
They feel no wear, they feel no tear,
They need no mending, no repair.

40
Life on its way returns into a mist,
Its quickness is its quietness again:
Existence of this world of things and men
Renews their never needing to exist.*

---

*The Way of Life According to Lao Tzu, Translated by Witter Bynner see copyright page for permission

Teachings of Mohammed

Mercy: "The Prophet said: 'Show mercy to those on earth so that He who is in heaven will have mercy on you'" (Sunan At-Tirmidhi)

All those who are in the heavens and the earth ask of Him; every moment He is in a state (of glory). Quran Chapter, Ar-Rahman, Verse 29, Shakir

Surely we have sent you with the truth as a bearer of good news and a warner, and there is not a people but a warner has gone among them. Quran, Fatir, Verse No.24, Maulana

Virtue: "The Prophet said: 'Do not be people without minds of your own, saying that if others treat you well you will treat them well, and that if they do wrong you will do wrong. Instead, accustom yourselves to do good if people do good and not to do wrong if they do evil'" (Sunan At-Tirmidhi).

God is the light of the heavens and the earth. A metaphor for His light is a niche in which there is a lamp placed in a glass. The glass is like a shining star which is lit from a blessed olive tree that is neither eastern nor western. Its oil almost lights up even though it has not been touched by the fire. It is light upon light. God guides to His light whomever He wants. God uses various metaphors. He has the knowledge of all things. Quran, Al-Noor Verse No:35, Rashad

Animals: "The Prophet said: 'Anyone who kills even a sparrow for no reason (should know that) it will cry aloud to Allah on the Day of the Resurrection, saying, "O my Lord! So-and-so killed me just for fun; he killed me for no reason!"'" (Sunan An-Nasa'i). "A'isha said: 'I was once riding a difficult (slow-moving) camel, so I kept hitting it. When the Prophet saw me, he said: "'Be gentle, for gentleness adorns everything in which it is found, and its absence leaves everything tainted.'"" (Musnad Ahmad).*

---

* Quotes from Mohammed, see copyright page for sources

We Come to Pray

During repentance, we come face-to-face with our harmful actions: We feel pain and guilt, sorrow and regret. Yet we know we are on the right path when we experience a deep cleansing of our heart, and conscience:

At a certain time and place
we come to pray.

We know why we are here:
it is to ask

to beseech the Most High
to forgive us.

Yet we have come
not only to pray

but with a deep need
to cry, to cleanse.

Opening our hearts
in this private place and time,
with the Most High our only witness,

our tears begin to flow
unchecked,

washing and emptying us
of everything

but a deep longing
for forgiveness,

and the absolute expectation
of acceptance.

And sometimes, in the emptiness
that follows our tears,

if we are lucky, a peaceful
Presence enters our room.

Gently it quiets our heart, comforting us
as surely as a mother's loving embrace.

And in this tender place and time
we are often shown

what we need to do—

to make right, our portion,
of the wrong.

Compassion and Justice

Somewhere inside of those who deliberately harm or steal, rape or kill, there has been a deep distortion of Love. Only this understanding can awaken within us a feeling of compassion.

For only with understanding and compassion are we able to forgive, and to pray for those who cause harm. Yet forgiveness does not mean an acceptance of dark deeds: actions based upon harm are not coming from the Most High, but arise within the shadow world of the human ego.

Thus alongside compassion for those who intentionally harm, rides an absolute knowledge of the promise of Divine Justice—that we know will never fail. This promise means that *we do not need to seek a personal revenge.*

Awareness of an ultimate, Divine Justice does not mean we shouldn't engage helpers, or the legal system when needed. It also does not mean that we should stay in the path of further harm. Yet it does mean that one day we can forgive their ignorance, and at some point offer them compassion—as we know, that sooner or later, the perfect Judgment of the Substance of Life will prevail—on this side, or the other:

Looking through eyes of Compassion
we can clearly See,

each person has done,
as they have done

according to the circumstances
they have lived.

Standing on this Wisdom base
we can not be easily swayed
by circumstance,

to seek a retribution through personal
revenge.

Instead we keep our faith and hearts
aligned with the Divine Promise:

"Vengeance Is Mine,
says the Most Supreme." *

---

* *Vengeance is mine and recompense, for the time they lose their footing; Because the day of their disaster is at hand and their doom is rushing upon them! Deuteronomy 32:35, NABRE*

The Holy Scripture of Nature

The words contained in our holy books are called scripture, and we have also heard that Nature has been called a scripture. How are these similar?

As we study our holy books we acquire, from youth, certain images and stories that arouse deep feelings, for the Holy Beings in our particular tradition. Our religious scripture thus becomes a central part of our lives. Carrying these deep feelings and images within us, whenever we read our holy books we experience the emotions and the awe, that our spiritual stream and family have passed down to us.

For example, a Christian, when reading in the New Testament about Christ, Mary and the disciples, or a Jew when reading in the Torah about Abraham and Sarah, or Moses and Miriam, may each be moved to tears. Yet would either of them respond in the same way if they were to read in the Quran, the holy book of the Muslims, about the life of Mohammed? Like this, we can also see that a Muslim may be moved to great bliss while reading the words of the Quran, and yet would not attain the same spiritual state as a Hindu will while reading the Bhagavad Gita.

In this way we can understand, that even though written forms of scripture evoke many beautiful images and feelings, the depth of these feelings are influenced by each one's culture and background, and training.

Thus it becomes easy for us to recognize the wondrous difference between the Holy Scripture of Nature, and the recorded scriptures of the world's religious traditions:

Nature carries the Living Essence of Life
directly to Her readers' hearts.

All are able to equally receive
Her Wisdom and Beauty,

without any words.

For the Holy Spirit is eternally Present,
is offered each moment anew, through
Nature's Living Gifts:

With no need for discourse,
Nature leads Her readers' hearts

beyond the content of intellect,
beyond recorded religious traditions,

into a Living Communion-Union—
with the One Heart of All.

A True Taste–Where All Differences Cease

All of the pleasures of the Earth and the heavens
are for human beings to enjoy.

How can we be tempted by the baubles of the world,
if we have ever experienced a True taste
of Nature's Majesty—

A glorious sunrise, shimmering with
deep violet and rose

Yellow-gold flowers, dancing in a soft breeze
wafting across a summer meadow

A cooling autumn rain, that brings
a sparkling rainbow—translucent
against silver-laced clouds

Falling asleep in a warm summer garden,
with no need to hurry anywhere...

Breathing in the vast, golden vista,
of a sun-swept desert, while relishing
our lover's grateful touch.

Immersed in Nature's Beauty, we lose the
"I" and the "Thou"

and when all such differences cease,
only Wonder is present,
only Joy abounds—

only Being
is Being.

Bringing Peace to the Table of Life

When those who claim to be seeking peace enter a peace conference, while holding in their hearts feelings of hatred or derision toward the other members, and in their minds the will for power over them, is there any shred of doubt that peace will prevail? Yet in this shameful way, mockery peace conferences are conducted all around the world.

The same false claims of striving for peace hold true for those who are fighting in religious wars, and are also true within the business world, and in our personal lives:

In order to have peace we must be peace,
we must bring peace with us

as our contribution to the
Table of Life.

We must carry peace with
us as our in-kind offering.

Otherwise we find, that
no matter how hungry
the human family is

for Beauty, for Love
and for Peace—

No one has brought to
the Table,
anything fit to eat.

The Purity of the Living World

Each infant is a holy teacher, as much as they are an ever-present student.

Typically by age two, a child's ego begins to establish itself as a separate entity from its mother and father. This is when the word "No!" emerges, and we know the sweet phase of babyhood is slipping away. Often the infant lets its caretakers know, ever so strongly, that they "Do! Not! Want! To be a Student! Right! Now!" Thus through loud, red-faced displays of displeasure, each toddler begins the struggle that leads them to attain separation, from their role as a dependent child, and begin to move into an independent, ego existence.

In our modern society, first as children and later as adults, we become separated not only from our parents and those around us, but also from the natural world. Once grown, if we ever try to get in touch with Nature's glory for a few precious days, and travel to the mountains or seaside, it is very difficult for us to unwind enough to fully experience, the deep peace that exists, within the Living Heart of the natural world.

Yet if we ever have a chance to merge ourselves, and enter the transcendent Beauty of Nature, our heart opens wide, and our Inner Being can touch, for a few moments at least, the 'brand-new view' of the world we experienced as a child—

In the Living Heart of Nature's world
we become enrapt in holiness,

and enter a place and time
of Divinity and Grace.

Our breath softens and deepens
and worldly thoughts dissolve,
as time slips away.

As Nature's scents and sounds surround us,
we want only to see,

only to touch, and be touched
by Her Beauty:

Standing on a wooden bridge,
above a crystal-clear, bubbling stream

sunlight caresses the leaves on the trees,
and our face—

and softly, amidst the pungent smells
of dampened Earth,

Her Living Presence completely fills
the place where we stand.

Oh, we remember this feeling…
it is why we have come!

Humbled, by the Sacredness we feel
our heart makes a promise,

as if the world could hear:

"I will not forget this Beauty, when I return to daily life!

I will come back—to this very place!

Oh yes, I must surely come again,

soon...

Oh so very soon."

Teachings of Paramahansa Yogananda

"The happiness of one's own heart alone cannot satisfy the Soul; one must try to include, as necessary to one's own true happiness, the happiness of others" [1]

I will help weeping ones to smile, by smiling myself, even when it is difficult. [2]

I will radiate love and goodwill to others so that I may open a channel for God's love to come to all. [3]

If you don't invite God to be your summer Guest, He won't come in the winter of your life. [4]

"Stillness is the altar of spirit." [5]

"Live quietly in the moment and see the beauty of all before you. The future will take care of itself......" [6]

"Dharma (cosmic law) aims at the happiness of all creatures." [7]

"The more deeply we perceive, the more striking becomes the evidence that a uniform plan links every form in manifold nature." [8]

If you permit your thoughts to dwell on evil, you yourself will become ugly. Look only for the good in everything so you absorb the quality of beauty. [9]

All quotes by Paramahansa Yogananda, from the following publications:
[1] Self-Realization magazine, Winter, 2000
[2,3] Metaphysical Meditations
[4, 5,6,7,8] Autobiography of a Yogi
[9] Spiritual Diary

"Make up your mind that you will be happy whether you are rich or poor, healthy or unhealthy, happily married or unhappily married, young or old, smiling or crying. Don't wait for yourself, your family, or your surroundings to change before you can be happy within yourself. Make up your mind to be happy within yourself, right now, whatever you are, or wherever you are." [10]

God is within and around me, protecting me, so I will banish the fear that shuts out His guiding light[11]

I am submerged in eternal light. It permeates every particle of my being. I am living in that light. The Divine Spirit fills me within and without.[12]

God is within and around me, protecting me, so I will banish the fear that shuts out His guiding light.[13]

All quotes by Paramahansa Yogananda, from the following publications:

[10] How to be happy all the time
[11,12, 13] Scientific Healing Affirmations

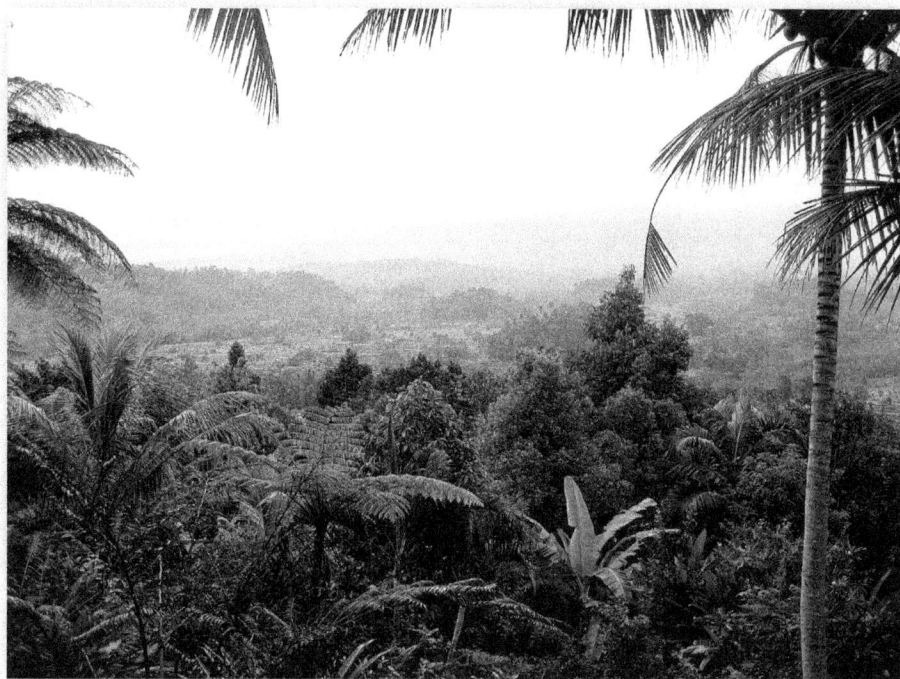

One

You shall know the Truth, and the Truth shall set you free.

Every Honor-bound Messenger has carried Truth, has spoken Truth. Every song they have sung, to all people, in the procession of Earthly time and experience, asks us, guides us all—to Be Love, to be living representatives of the One Source of Life—

All of the prayers, from all lips
throughout the whole world,
are prayed to that One

All harm done to anyone
is done to that One

111

All Beauty and Love given to anyone
is given to that One

Flesh that is wounded on anyone
has wounded that One

Kindness given to anyone, or anything at all,
is given to that One

Words of hatred spoken to anyone
are spoken to that One

Plots to destroy, and all destruction,
destroy a part of that One

Beautiful works of art and architecture,
are created for the enjoyment
of that One

And all that has ever existed is One—
with-in the One Breath, of the Only One.

This is Truth.

And when we have ears to hear this,
and when we can Realize this Truth,

Our thoughts and actions
and our very lives, will be in harmony

With the Holy Messengers and Saints,
of the Ever-Living One.

Surviving by Grace

Flowers do not bloom before the snows
and frosts have set the stage for Spring.

Likewise, we find that the greatest
gifts given to humanity,

those of religion, music, poetry,
and many other forms

of art...

and Love,

have most often been birthed by Souls
somehow enabled by Grace,

to first bear,
and then to survive

the longest, coldest,
and darkest of winters.

The Garden of Eden Still Exists

Love, the Essence of Life, the primal element of the Most Holy, is indelibly imprinted upon each and every heart.

The Divine Essence of Love exists with-in all life. Knowledge of this depth and presence of Love is what each prophet and poet is called to bring to humanity, and what every Soul hopes to attain. And no matter the path, Beauty is what each Soul knows to be the rock bottom foundation—upon which Love, and all that exists, rests:

Our search for the Essence of Love
might begin one morning

while looking at Reality as a Sacred,
Holy Mirror,

anticipating—that at any moment
Beauty will appear.

Carrying this thought as a seed,
letting it permeate our core

we drink in a radiant sunrise
while the sweet scent of honeysuckle
fills the air.

Our shining Heart-Light
radiates through our Being,

and anything our illuminated eyes
chance to rest upon

becomes as Beauty-filled,
as we are able to perceive.

A sudden spark of Inspiration
brings us to tears—

The Garden of Eden still exists
right here on Earth,

whenever we, Her stewards,
are able to stand as Witness.

Teachings of Jesus

'Teacher, which [is] the greatest command in the Law?' Jesus
said to him, 'Thou shalt love the Lord thy God with all thy heart,
and with all thy soul, and with all thine understanding –this is the first
and greatest command; and the second [is] like to it, Thou shalt love
thy neighbor as thyself; on these two commands all the law and
the Prophets do hang.'

Love does no harm to a neighbor. Therefore, Love is the fulfillment
of the law.

If those who lead you say to you, "Look, the kingdom is in the sky!"
then the birds of the sky will precede you. If they say to you, "It is
in the sea," then the fishes will precede you.

Rather, the kingdom is inside of you, and outside of you.
When you come to know yourselves, then you will be known, and you
will realize that you are the children of the Living Creator. But if you do
not come to know yourselves, then you exist in poverty, and you are poverty.

So in everything, do to others what you would have them do to you, for
this sums up the law and the Prophets.

For there is no good tree that brings forth rotten fruit; nor again a rotten
tree that brings forth good fruit. For each tree is known by its own fruit. For
people don't gather figs from thorns, nor do they gather grapes from a
bramble bush.

A prophet is not without honor, except in his own country, and among his
own relatives, and in his own house.

What Are We Really Doing Here

What are we doing here, really?
Have we come here to make money?

Have we come to make families who make
money, and war,
and despoil the Earth

with the ways and things that the power of
money creates?

Have we come to follow religious leaders,
who vilify and demand that we harm
or we kill,

those who do not believe, or pray
as we do?

A collective response arises from our hearts:

"No! We know this is not why we have come!
We have come for a higher purpose,
been sent by Divine decree

to bring Love and not hate,
joy and not harm,

and to glorify Creation—
that is why we have come!"

Yet when religious leaders claim
the Most High exists only within
our church, our mosque, or temple walls—

our religious paths have become deformed,
are no longer able to honestly Serve
the All-in-All.

For the Most High cannot be confined
by man-made walls, or ideologies,

but lives with-in all people
all nations, all cultures

and Calls us to Love one another
twenty-four hours a day,

from the Eternal Temple,
in the center, of every heart.

A Hidden Paradise

When our eyes and our ears are truly open, all things are known as Sacred, all people are seen as manifestations of the Most High.

As we awaken, all things, in fact the very ground we walk upon, become known as holy, including all people, animals, plants, and elements. The stars and the planets are also understood to have been created by, and filled with, the One Source, the Substance of Life—

Imagine the incredible Joy the Saints and
Prophets experience,

Knowing intimately, as they do,
the Presence of the Most High—

With each step, and each breath they take,
they look upon the world with open Eyes,
Hear with open Ears.

In fact, our lives appear as pages in a book
they can easily read.

Imagine, if you will, that we could See
and Hear as clearly as they—

what treasures we would find!

Instead our lives mostly
tell the same sad story:

Humanity remains asleep
in a shadow-filled world,

unaware, that each moment we exist
in an unobserved,

and thus hidden from view—
Eternal Paradise!

Why We Praise

Whenever we are moved to praise, Love and Light have entered our world.

Praise comes upon us when we are not even
thinking about it, the instant our eyes
catch sight of a rainbow.

Praise certainly occurs whenever we see
the sweet smile of an infant.

And we know, for sure, praise will happen when
our heart is filled with Joy, listening to a
beautiful piece of music,

or while we are paying homage
to a brilliant, evening sky.

At wonder-filled moments like these we
feel our Spirit get ready to soar!

For when Beauty Calls, oh we gladly fly—
as high as we are able,
while our heart is opened wide!

And, in these Light-filled frames,
as we stand transfixed—

we are moved, once again,
to praise.

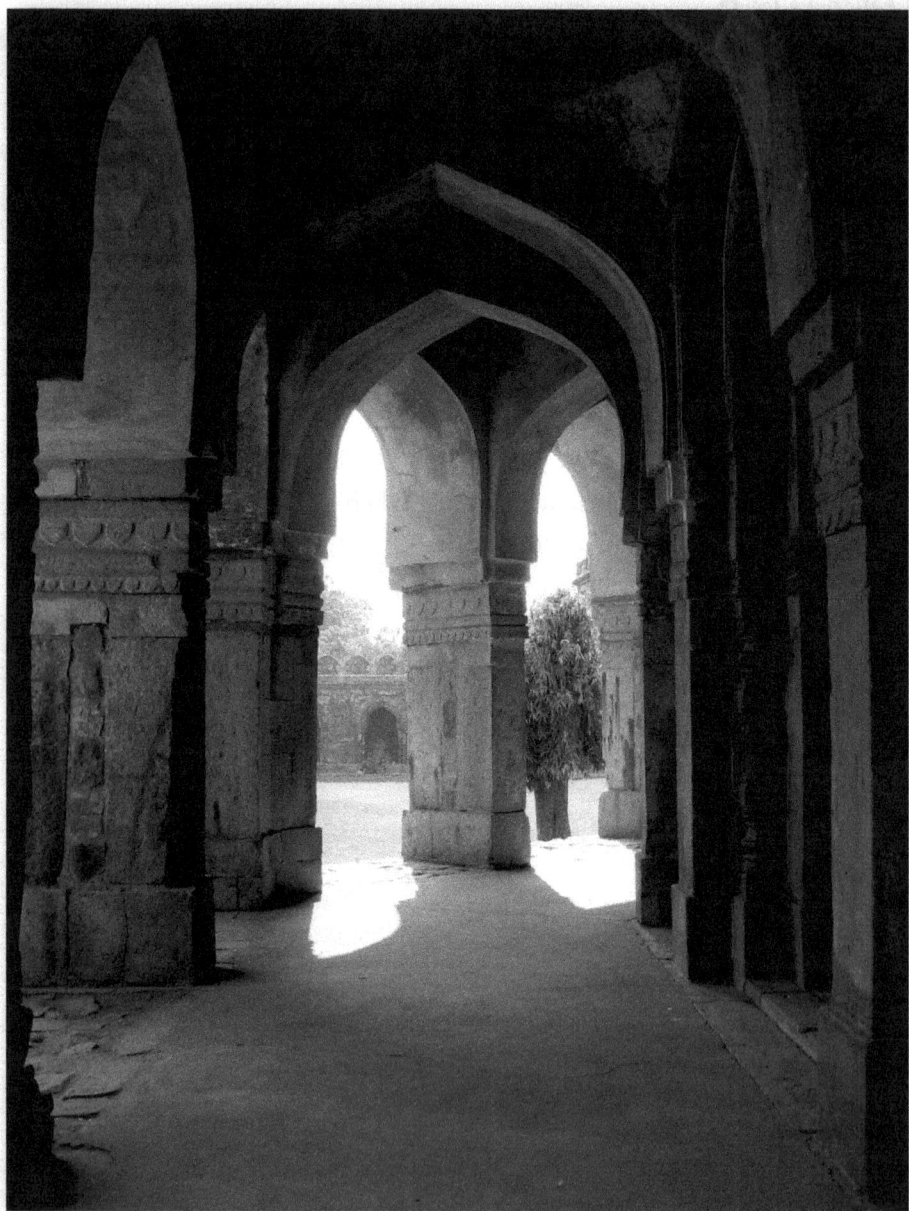

Purifying Our Bubble and the World

Many people claim that all things are possible in this Reality: If we just 'think we can,' or if we 'pray hard enough,' whatever we want can occur. In fact, some will say if we 'believe strongly enough,' or if we 'become pure enough,' we can attain the never-ending State of Grace.

A question arises: "Is it possible to capture, to live a life of Perfect Awareness, to walk with Peace into each moment, and, no matter how hard the storms rage around us, to carry with us the space and time of Nirvana, the State of Living Grace, like the Saints, and the Buddha—all day and all night long?" If this were possible, how contented would we be, living in our own insulated, protective bubble of purity, separated from all darkness in the world, by an impenetrable aura of bliss, throughout our days and nights.

A second question might help us find our answer: "If one were to enter a desert and place a potted plant of tender violets on the sand in the heat of the noonday sun, and leave it there for a whole week, do you think it would survive?"

In these questions we can see that there are fantasies, and there are realities that exist in our physical world. Rather than living in a state of absolute stillness and perfection, separated from the world, our lives are immersed, interlaced in a flowing stream of life, that changes with each moment. And it seems that even those many look to as examples of steadiness and Divinity, have lost their persona of peacefulness during times of stress:

Job cursed his day
Moses lost his temper, struck a rock, and killed
Sarah experienced jealousy
Jesus became angry at the moneychangers in the synagogue
Mohammed, fearing for his life, fled to Medina
Siddhartha, the Buddha became angry with his teacher.

There are many other examples of our role models of Divinity, losing their faith. Thankfully, though they experienced harsh feelings, and inhumane situations associated with their trials, the Beloved Messengers, Saints and Prophets, remained true to their vows to the Most High.

Like the great ones, we spend our lives striving for balance every day. If we choose to use these Divine Ones as examples of how to live our lives, when we watch their efforts, for themselves and their whole world, we see that when they fell down they struggled to rise again, and return to their fields, to plow and to plant. Their goal was all-Ways, "Let me be of Service to All." Thus the ancient teaching becomes perfectly clear: "I am a bubble, make me the sea!"*

---

* Quote "I am a bubble, make me the sea." Paramahansa Yogananda, Cosmic Chants

Beneath All Walls, Creation Calls

Knowledge and experience of our Union with the Most High is the birthright of each and every Soul.

Our Union with the Most Supreme, though hidden in our modern world, only needs a seeking heart to uncover—the reality of who and what we are:

Learning from one's youth
there are those who are the in-casts

and those who are the out-casts,

creates artificial walls
based not only upon the categories

of what Creator one prays to
or does not pray to,

but also upon one's color,
physical, intellectual, and social structure.

And as long as these, or any such
artificially created estrangements

exist as invisible walls
between us,

how can we ever hope to bring
to Light and to Life

the Reality of our nobility,

and inviolable Union,
with the All-in-All.

The One Orchestra

"I call Heaven and Earth to witness against you today, that I have set before you life and death, the blessing and the curse. So choose life in order that you may live, you and your descendants." — Deuteronomy, 30:19

The One Orchestra includes—

all things
all beings
all time, and no time
all religions all beliefs
all understandings
all actions
all wars
all warriors
all peace.

And each one is a warrior.

And it is through all of the thoughts,
all desires,

and each of the actions
of all of the warriors—

that the Supreme Lives and Breathes,
and the Universe becomes well-tuned.

And it is the process of becoming well-tuned
that ultimately creates the promised land,

the Garden of Eden, both here and there:
'As in Heaven, so on Earth.'

The Real Currency of Life

Those who possess the Real Currency of Life are the true billionaires of the world.

Forms of currency for goods and services, as well as all things that are considered desirable, change within each culture and epoch. This shows that everything based upon material things is transitory. Yet there is one form of currency whose value has remained unchanged, throughout all time—

We all flow within the One Being, the Source of Love-Light and Life. And, everyone, in every climb, though they may have little of the present-day form of legal tender, always has abundant access to the Real Currency of Life:

With no need for plotting
cheating or strife,

the Real currency of Life flows freely
to and from, and in between,
each and every heart.

Brought to life through
the Sustainer, the Maintainer
the Bestower of Sustenance,

everyone who has ever lived Knows
this highest form of currency

does not change in value during times of
scarcity or abundance, or even the state
of the stock market.

In fact, it can neither be bartered
or sold—

not with silver or gold,
nor jewels or loans.

And what is this priceless form of exchange
with us since the beginning of time?

The Real Currency of Life is Love,
and Love alone.

Nature's Beauty Will Take You Home

A Walk in the Garden…

A drop of dew shimmers and shines
upon a soft petal of a fragrant rose—
all thoughts of the world and self vanish!

Sunset, upon the horizon of a calm blue ocean,
warm sand, salt air, the sky glows yellow and pink—
one's being absolutely full, exclaims, 'O Beauty! O Grace!'

There is, within Nature's Bounty
a stillness—so precious, so pervading

that whenever we are caught by one
of Her treasures, or pause to be with Her glory

we are drawn within Her holiness,
longing only to taste Her fullness—

to follow Her fragrant paths of peace
all the way to their Source.

This sense of following,
of merging ourselves into Nature's Essence,

may be likened to intimate moments of
unhurried lovemaking,

a feeling there is something more
to be Known

a part of ourselves we have yet
to explore,

where something timeless
and wonderful awaits,

and we have no doubt—

if we can only be still enough
present enough, soft enough,

if we can only follow
deeply enough,

intertwining ourselves within Her
Grand Beauty

we will find it—

we will most certainly arrive
at our home.

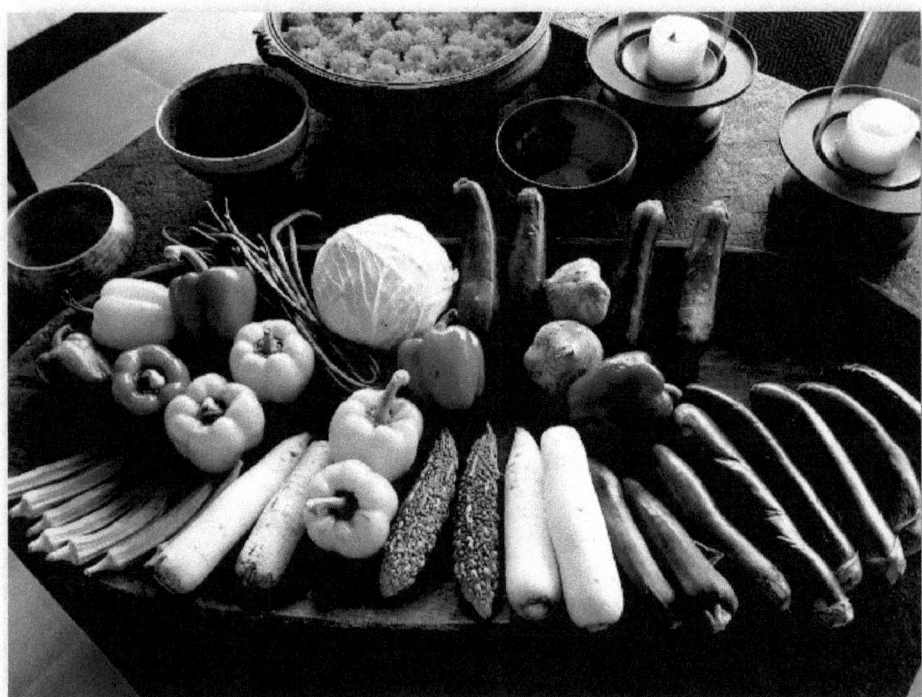

Make the Best of Today

Making the best of today means, as much as possible, keeping ourselves within the great peace available to all, each moment.

It is written that Jesus said to those who came to him for healing, "Go in peace, your faith has made you whole." On one level, we find that he is relinquishing any portion of the healing, and is instead turning the seeker's face toward the Most High. Yet, if we look at his Message from another point of view, we find that he is reminding those who seek Divine assistance, that all positive results from Gifts of healing, rest within our own minds and hearts.

For even though one's faith may be strong while standing in front of their chosen healer, if one begins to doubt the healing they receive, their illness has a good chance of returning. This is because healers can only assist us on our journey: we have to somehow find within ourselves, an Inner connection to the health we seek.

And though a person be near to death, persecuted or imprisoned, it is always possible to enter one's heart, speak directly with the Most High, and find a Gift of healing Love-Light that can brighten up, even one's darkest of days.

The Beloved Lives

The Beloved Lives.
The Beloved Lives within.
The Beloved Lives within the Hearts of all.

Inside of the eyes and the hearts of those
we have chosen to isolate or hate,

and for the soldiers or terrorists,
inside of those they have been
sent to kill—

The Beloved Lives.

We know this Truth whenever we find ourselves
quickly turning our face aside

trying to forget, as
soon as possible—

the look in their eyes—and the pain,
of those who have been harmed

in thought, word or deed

by ourselves,
and an unawakened world.

Yet though we try to forget we find
that our heart does not easily

'Let us forget.'

For our Conscience belongs not to us,
but the Most Supreme

Who Sees and Knows all things—

with Eyes that never tire,
never sleep.

The Divine Message of the Golden Rule

Baha'i Faith
Lay not on any Soul a load that you would not wish
to be laid upon you, and desire not for anyone the things
you would not desire for yourself.
~~~~~~~~~~~~~~~~~~~~~~

Brahmanism
This is the sum of duty: do naught unto others
which would cause you pain if done to you.
~~~~~~~~~~~~~~~~~~~~~~

Buddhism
Hurt not others in ways that you yourself would find hurtful.
A state that is not pleasing or delightful to me,
how could I inflict that upon another?
~~~~~~~~~~~~~~~~~~~~~~

Christianity
Do unto others as you would have them do unto you.
~~~~~~~~~~~~~~~~~~~~~~

Confucianism
Do not impose on others what you yourself do not desire.
~~~~~~~~~~~~~~~~~~~~~~

Hinduism
Do not do to others what would cause pain if done to you.
~~~~~~~~~~~~~~~~~~~~~~

Islam
No one of you is a believer until he desires for his brother
that which he desires for himself.
~~~~~~~~~~~~~~~~~~~~~~

Jainism
One should treat all creatures in the world as one would like to be treated.
~~~~~~~~~~~~~~~~~~~~~~

Judaism
What is hateful to you, do not do to your neighbor. This is the entire Law.
All the rest is commentary...Thou shalt love thy neighbor as thyself.
~~~~~~~~~~~~~~~~~~~~~~

Native American Spirituality
Respect for all life is the foundation. (The Great Law of Peace)
~~~~~~~~~~~~~~~~~~~~~~

Paganism
The law imprinted on the hearts of all people is to love
the members of society as themselves.
~~~~~~~~~~~~~~~~~~~~~~

Shintoism
Hurt not others with that which pains yourself. The heart
of the person before you is a mirror. See there your own form.
~~~~~~~~~~~~~~~~~~~~~~

Sikhism
Don't create enmity with anyone as the Most High is within everyone.
~~~~~~~~~~~~~~~~~~~~~~

Sufism
If you haven't the will to gladden someone's heart, then at least
beware lest you hurt someone's heart—for no sin exists but this.
~~~~~~~~~~~~~~~~~~~~~~

Taoism
A sound person's heart is not shut within itself, but is open
to other people's hearts: I feel the heartbeats of others above my own.
~~~~~~~~~~~~~~~~~~~~~~

Unitarianism
We affirm and promote respect for the interdependent web
of all existence of which we are a part.
~~~~~~~~~~~~~~~~~~~~~~

Wicca
Do whatever you want to, as long as it harms
nobody, including yourself.
~~~~~~~~~~~~~~~~~~~~~~

Yoruba (Nigeria)
One going to take a pointed stick to pinch a baby bird
should first try it on himself to feel how it hurts.

~~~~~~~~~~~~~~~~~~~~~~~

Zoroastrianism
Do not do unto others whatever is injurious to yourself.
That nature alone is good which refrains from doing unto
another whatsoever is not good for itself.

~~~~~~~~~~~~~~~~~~~~~~~

Appendix

An Old Yet New Translation of the Shema

אֶ|חָד יְהוָה אֱ|לֹ|הֵי|נוּ יְהוָה אֵל|יִשְׂ רָ שְׁ מַ ע

(2)	(1)	(1)	(4)	(3)	(2)	(1)	(1)	(3)	(2)	(1)	(2)	(1)
e·chad		Adonai		e·lo·**hey**·nu			Adonai		yis·ra·el		she·ma'	
one LORD				our God (is)			The LORD		O Israel		Hear!	

Hear, O Israel: The LORD our God, the LORD is one. (Deut 6:4)

Shema

"Shema Yisrael YaHuVah! Eloheinu YaHuVah! Ehad!"

Hear!

Understand!

Guard these words

And act upon them.

Struggle to Remember

The Divine Presence of the Universe.

Our Oneness is bound together, throughout eternity.

Oh Remember, Divine Being

The One Breath of the Universe.

Amen

Translating the Shema

The Shema is one of only two prayers in the Torah that are commanded by the Most High. The other is the the other is Birkat Ha-Mazon, the grace after meals. The Shema must be recited twice each day, upon rising in the morning and before going to bed each night. Many religious Jews say it three times a day, along with their other prayers. It is included in most religious services, morning and evening.

The Hebrew word, Shema means to 'Listen', or 'Hear." The Shema has three passages. For this translation we will be focusing only on the first:

Shema

Shema Yisrael Adonai Eloheinu Adonai Echad

"Hear O Israel, The Lord is our God, the Lord is One

Hebrew letters and words have many meanings, and at a certain time I wanted to see if there was a deeper meaning to the translation of this sacred saying. After much research, I compiled a new translation from looking into the various meanings of each letter and word. I have listed below these various meanings so you can follow how I arrived to this translation. And you will also find links to a few of the many resources I used.

The Words, And the Meanings Each of the Words Contain

First we can review the meaning of the word Adonai, and see that the Hebrew letters as written do not say the word, "Adonai" even though the the common way that people read and speak the Shema is as if they did:

Shema Yisrael Adonai Eloheinu Adonai Echad

These six words are spoken when reciting the Shema. The letters for the third word, are: Y, H, V, H. Yet they are not pronounced that way in traditional Jewish Synagogues or Temples. The reason these letters have remained silent, and are replaced with the word, "Adonai", (Lord) is that the exact pronunciation of the vowels connected to these four consonants have been lost. However many Jews, Christians and others have come to add vowel sounds to these four letters, and thus we have the words, YaHoVah, or YaHuWeh, YaHuVah being used to pronounce this holy name of God. I have chosen to keep the vowel sounds, 'YaHuVah' for this translation. The reason is that in the Torah and Bible many of the names of the ancient people used the sounds, YaHu as a name that represents the Most High, and this was added to people's names, as a way of honoring the Creator (see below). As for using the sound, Vah, Vav, as V, is used as a (consonent) and as ow/uw is a vowel and I decided on the more commonly used sound of 'Vah.' though either pronounciation will not change the translation.

Here is a summary of my research for the "Old Yet New Translation" of the Shema.

Meanings of the Words

Shema: To hear, to listen, but also to understand, to guard, to nail down with nails, and to then act upon by following with righteousness.

Yisrael: Those who struggle to remember; To ensure the Divine Essence prevails upon the world.

Eloheinu: El: Authority, power; Our Creator; Elohai, My God; Eloah, Ruach: Feminine, Goddess, the One Breath that creates the Universe: "Eloah is Hebrew feminine singular, and is a name of the Goddess. In Job, 27:3 he states: "All the while the spirit of the Most High, Ruach, Eloah, (the Breath of the Most High) is in my nostrils"

Echad: Oneness which is produced through activity; 'Uniting separate threads'; To be 'bound together', like cords in a rope; To unite, to join together, to be a unity.

The Letters: Y*H*V*H* - Here we will see that each letter itself has deep meanings.

"And they shall place My name upon the sons of Israel, and I shall respect them." Numbers 6:27

Y:Yod: The spark of the Spirit in everything; Every Hebrew letter contains a Yod; Every page of a Torah would be considered invalid without a Yod.

The letter Yod is the first letter of the Divine Name. The sound of YAH became a part of the name of the ancient Prophets, as well as ordinary people. Also interesting about this adding of YAH to a name is that traditionally the Most High was believed to exist within each and every person, and all being. Thus in order to honor the Most High, whenever people met each other they would add YAH to their name to say hello, so that the Most High would be also acknowledged, as living within them. A Yod was also added as a permanent prefix or suffix to names, for example, Mari-yah— Maria; or Mari-yah-m, Miri-yah-m. We see below that many people's names in the Bible had "Yah" and also "YaHu" attached to their names, and this can serve us with regard to the pronunciation of the holy name, YHVH:

YAH: "It is I". The word "Yah" was used alone as the name of the Divine One, the Most High, also YaHu: Here are some examples of names with "Yah", and "Yahu".

YAHU: The root of YHVH as well as "YA" and "YAHU" is literally, "To Breathe"

Yah'akov (Jacob)

Yah-Hu-Dah =Judah = This name is a good one for us to use as we look at the pronunciation of YHVH, as the letter Dalet, D, is the only difference == Yah-Hu, Yah-Hu-Da, Ya-Hu-Vah

Yedi-di-Yah (Jedidiah=Solomon) — (Loved by Yah)

Eli-Yah, Eli-Ya-Hu Eliyahu (E-Li-Yah, Elijah) Note: there is no J in Hebrew) — (My Creator is Yah) (My authority is The One who has Breath)

Yeria-Yah – (Yeriah) A curtain that is in the tabernacle, fastened by a silver hook to a pole, and a sheet of parchment in a Torah scroll

Yesha'Yah-Hu, (IsaiYah) — Isaiah — (YaHu is salvation)

Yirme-Yah or Yirme-YaHu (Jeremiah) — (Raised up by Yah) Note: there is no J in Hebrew)

Ova-di-Yah, Oba-di-Yah — Obadiah — (Servant of Yah)

Ze-cha-ri-Yah (Zechariah) — (Remembered by Yah)

Yah-Hu-Sha-fat —Josephat — (YaHu is Judge)

Mar-i-Yah, Miri-Yahm — Maria, Miryam, Miriam — (I Am Yah, in Aramaic, I Am the Most High),

Yah-Hu-Na-tan — Jonathan — (YaHu has given)

Ne-tan-Yah-Hu — Netanyahu, Israel's Prime Minister

Hal-le-lu-Yah —Halleluyah — (All praise Yah)

Ali-Yah— Aliyah — (Going up to God)

HEY: The Divine name contains two H letters. Hey means: The breath of the Divine's mouth, the out breathing of being; the Light of and the creation of the Universe; the Presence of the Divine in the human heart: "It is I"; Used as we saw above with the sound of HU.

VAV: Connecting; Joining heaven and earth; Between spiritual and creation; a Divine hook that binds things together; Each page of a Torah scroll has a VAV that begins the page, 'hooking' it, binding it to the page before; "Being" Choosing to pronounce as a "V" or "W" will not change the meaning of this letter, or the translation.

The Shema, An Interfaith Prayer

As you can see this most holy prayer, the Shema, to be carried in the heart and prayed two times or more each day, takes on a much deeper meaning when read with this 'old yet new' translation. Using the inner meanings of the Hebrew words and letters as a guide, we can imagine how deeply saying the Shema must have affected the ancient people, so much more than our abbreviated version today.

When they prayed the Shema and taught its meaning to their children, all the while they held in their hands and hearts its underlying Message. Seen this way it is really a beautiful universal prayer, for all people, all nations. If we carry these thoughts with us, how much the world would be moved toward peace. Perhaps you might want to try it out for a week or so, and see how it feels to you.

Sources: Here are a few links that I hope will be easy to locate online to get you started. There are many scholarly sources available, and others I have used, yet these have compiled valuable and detailed information about the Hebrew letters, their meanings, and the meanings of the words in the Shema.

The Hebrew Alphabet, Learning the Hebrew Consonants —
http://www.hebrew4christians.com/Grammar/Unit_One/Aleph-Bet/aleph-bet.html

Ancient Hebrew Research Center, Ploughing Through History From the Aleph to the Tav — ancient-hebrew.org

Hebrew Alphabet for Dummies 6 - Advanced —
http://zionism-israel.com/hebrew/Hebrew_Alphabet_for_Dummies_6a.htm

Katia's Esoteric Christianity Blog, God-the-Mother Wrongly Removed from Jewish & Christian Teachings, p.33 — https://www.northernway.org/weblog/?p=33

Photography Credits

All photographs in this book are original images by Emi Miller except as noted herein:

Three Faiths Declaring the One Creator
Heart Clouds Over New Mexico

The Golden Rule, Given to All Paths, All Ways
Ceremony Day, Eva Rose Edleson

Unerringly Guided Toward Perfection
Good Morning Rose, Eva Rose Edleson

Love's Harvest
Angel Grove in Redwood Forest

Your Beauty Eyes Are Needed
Reflections in a Sunset Pond

Crosses All Borders
In the Pink, Eve Rose Edleson

The Alpha and the Omega, the Circle of Life
A Summer Porch

When the Heart Becomes Open in Prayer
Nature's Beauty Lake, Emi Miller, permission to publish:
Meher Spiritual Center, Inc.

Love Is One With Truth
A Gift of Love, Eva Rose Edleson

Louder Than Words
Sweet Fruit, Eva Rose Edleson

Your Journey to Truth Begins Here
Deer in Morning Light

Our Only Task
Beauty's Gift

Our Union with Purity
Spring Morning Blooming

One Creator, One Breath
High Mesa Mountain Sky, Eva Rose Edleson

This Is the Plan
Birnbeck pier at Weston-super-Mare, Somerset,
Nick Whetstone

Our Own Hearts and Hands
The Heart of a Strawberry

Guidance Arrives
A Starving Mother, New Delhi

Teachings of Mother Teresa
The Water Gatherer

Winning the Sacred Gift of Life
Tibetan Woman Elder, Image Copyright James Wheeler, 2013,
used under license from SouvenirPixels.com.

The Cooking Pot
Firing the Pot, Eva Rose Edleson

Teachings of Avatar Meher Baba
Going Up, Emi Miller, permission to publish,
Meher Spiritual Center, Inc.

Realizing Our Oneness
A Summer Walk in Nature

Until the Circle Is Whole
The Mother Temple, Pura Besakih, largest and most
revered temple, on the slopes of Gunung Agung Bali

High-Ways of Love and Light and Life
With Light

The Eternal Wheel of Life
Creation Work, Eva Rose Edleson

When All Life Has Voice
Mountain Meadow with Flowers, Eva Rose Edleson

We Come to Pray
Purple Iris after a Morning Rain

The Holy Scripture of Nature
Quantocks, Nick Whetstone

A True Taste—Where All Differences Cease
Camel and Fish Clouds over Mountains

Bringing Peace to the Table of Life
Fallen Soldiers

One
In the Mists of Beauty

The Garden of Eden Still Exists
Roadside Spring Flowers

A Hidden Paradise
On the Way

Purifying Our Bubble and the World
Passage-Way, India

Beneath All Walls, Creation Calls
Morning Mist On Mountain

The Real Currency of Life
Early Morning, Downtown

Nature's Beauty Will Take You Home
Bali Mountains

Make the Best of Today
Harvest, Eva Rose Edleson

The Beloved Lives
Standing for Goodness and Truth, Eva Rose Edleson

The Divine Message of the Golden Rule
A Circle of Friends

About the Author

For more than forty years Emi Miller has dedicated her life to seeking wisdom from the world's religious and spiritual traditions. During this time she has developed and led interfaith peace circles, meditation, sound and breath-work seminars, and healing prayer services throughout the United States. She is a Licensed Acupuncturist, NCCAOM Certified, Asian Bodywork Therapist, and a traditional Naturopath. She is a Registered Nurse, a Certified Holistic Nurse, and an Interfaith, Stephen Minister. She has owned and managed an Integrative, Holistic Health practice for twenty-five years. Miller has taught classes in universities, private and public schools and hospitals to nursing and medical students, as well as natural medicine students, practitioners, and the public, and has published many Integrative Medicine, interfaith and spirituality articles, in professional journals, magazines and newsletters. She currently leads a poetry critique group, and has had a world-wide following of her writings posted on her public and private websites, for 17 years.

She is currently working on the second and third volumes of *In Wisdom's Light*. You can contact her through her websites:

www.emispoetryandprose.dreamhosters.com
www.integrativeholistichealth.org

www.ingramcontent.com/pod-product-compliance
Lightning Source LLC
Chambersburg PA
CBHW060014050426
42448CB00012B/2749